TECHNOLOGY TIPS FOR LAWYERS AND OTHER BUSINESS PROFESSIONALS

JEFFREY ALLEN AND ASHLEY HALLENE

AMERICAN BAR ASSOCIATION
Solo, Small Firm and
General Practice Division

Cover design by Elmarie Jara/ABA Design

Printed in the United States of America.

20 19 18 17 16   5 4 3 2 1

Library of Congress Cataloging-in-Publication Data

CIP Data is on file with the Library of Congress.

Discounts are available for books ordered in bulk. Special consideration is given to state bars, CLE programs, and other bar-related organizations. Inquire at Book Publishing, ABA Publishing, American Bar Association, 321 N. Clark Street, Chicago, Illinois 60654-7598.

www.ShopABA.org

Contents

Introduction. vii

Hardware and Equipment. 1
  Carry a Cellular Hotspot. 3
  E-readers versus Tablets 4
  Laser Multifunction Printers. 5
  Cover Your Keyboard 6
  Bose Soundlink III 7
  Bose Soundlink Mini II. 8
  Bose Noise-Canceling Headphones 9
  Set Up a Functional Storage Plan 10
  Seagate Wireless Plus Mobile Storage 11
  Hover Cam Mini 5 12
  Visit the Colonel! (No, Not the Chicken Guy) 13
  Get a Tablet 14
  Take Your iPad to Court 15
  Portable Hard Drives 16
  Logitech Ultrathin Keyboard iPad Cover 17
  Mophie Juice Packs. 18
  Present Like a Pro with a Wireless Presenter 19
  Get a Mac! 20
  Adonit Jot Fine Point Stylus 21
  Grid-It 22
  Get a Good Scanner 23
  Build Your Own Cloud Storage: Cloudstor and Pogoplug. 24
  Build Your Own Cloud Storage: Drobo Transporter. 25
  Protect Your Mobile Displays 26

Software. 29
  Adobe Acrobat 31
  Firm Central. 32
  Mozilla Firefox 34
  Mind Maps. 35
  Electronic Trial Notebooks 36
  Some Common Microsoft Shortcuts 37
  Doodle 39
  Google Scholar 40
  CodeTwo Outlook Attachment Reminder 41

ConceptDraw Office 3 42
DEVONthink 43
CLIO 44
Microsoft Office 365 45
FileMaker Pro 47
Credenza 48
Send a Fax without a Fax Machine 49

Security and Ethics **51**
Metadata: Know What You Are Sending in Microsoft Word . . . 52
Password Protect 54
Your Devices, Information, and Files 54
Use Strong Passwords 54
Keep Your Passwords Secure 55
Use Biometric Security 56
1Password 56
Password Meter 57
How Secure Is My Password? 57
Stop Using TrueCrypt 57
Limit Your Exposure: Avoid Public Wi-Fi 59
You Need Privacy When You Work 61
Enable Auto-Lock and Add a Passcode 63
Turn Off Bluetooth When Not in Use 65
Protect against Cell Phone Viruses 66
Keep Your Software Up to Date 67
Back Up Essential Files 69
Encrypt Important and Confidential Data 71
Redundancy Is Not Always Bad 72
DocuSign 73
Security on the Go 74
Prevent Identity Theft: Use Apple Pay 75
Crack Down on Spam in Your Inbox 76

Travel Tips **79**
FareCompare 80
FlightBoard 81
Flight Update Pro 82
TripIt 83
Buy Smart 84
Go Better with GOES 85
Gate Guru 87

Miscellaneous Tips **89**
  The Art of Mobile Lawyering 90
  Blogging Is Good 91
  ... Blogging with Graphics Is Better. 93
  Embrace the Cloud. 94
  Keep in Sync with Dropbox. 95
  The Pomodoro Technique 96
  Amazon.com and Other Online Shopping Sites 97
  Store Data in the Cloud. 99
  Get a Handwriting Font 100
  Create an Inexpensive Electronic Signature. 101
  Ruby Receptionists 102
  Use Electronic Business Cards 104
  URL Shorteners 105
  Develop Timelines for Trial Use 106
  Use Flowcharts. 107
  Write Better E-mails 109
  Save Yourself from That "Oh No" Moment with E-mail. 110
  Update Your Wireless Accounts 112
  Hire an Inexpensive Editor: WordRake 113
  Beware of LinkedIn Endorsements and Recommendations . . 114
  Outsource Typing 115
  Use Outlook's Follow-Up Reminder 116
  Organize Your Digital Files 117
  Make Your Website "Mobile Friendly". 118
  Move Your iTunes Library to an External Drive. 119
  Google Search Tips. 120
  Atwitter about Twitter?. 121
  Fitbit 122
  Any.do 123
  Trello 124
  Get Our Books 125

Introduction

The importance of technology in our professional and personal lives continues to grow at an ever-increasing rate. Courts have moved toward recognizing a duty for attorneys to acquire a level of basic competence in dealing with technology. The ABA Model Rules have recognized that duty in some areas for several years. Attorneys have learned and are learning that technology can help them practice more efficiently and effectively. As a result, more and more attorneys have grown increasingly interested in learning about technology.

We have done programs presenting tips on technology and practice for many years in locations all over the country. We have also written about technology for lawyers for many years. We often get questions about our tips programs. Sometimes the questions come from people who attended a program or read an article but want additional information. Many times we get questions from those who could not attend a show, asking about topics we covered or requesting copies of the slide show.

We thoroughly enjoy doing those programs and writing those articles. We were delighted when the GPSolo Division asked us to create this book for the division to highlight some of the most popular and important tips we have addressed in our work over the last year. We were even more pleased when they told us that they would like to have us prepare a new edition of the book every year or so covering the new material we brought into our programs.

We have tried to present the tips in this book as we would in a program. We do not go into great detail as to any of the tips or recommendations. We present them briefly to introduce the information or the product to you for further investigation or consideration. We anticipate that some of you may have heard some of the tips before, perhaps at one of our presentations or in one of our articles. We expect that many of you will find much of the information in this book new to you. We also anticipate that many of the tips in this book will prove useful to most attorneys in their professional life, their personal life, or both.

We hope that you will enjoy this book and the style of presentation we use for the tips. We anticipate that this book will be the start of a relationship with many readers, who will look forward to each new edition of the book to see what new information they can get, what new technology we have learned about, and what new software and hardware might prove useful to them.

We hope that you will get some tips in this book and in our future editions that will help you in your professional and personal lives by making things easier for you to accomplish, making you more efficient or more effective as an attorney, or making your life a little bit easier. Please note that while we have endeavored to organize the tips into logical groupings in each chapter, there is some overlap in that some tips fit in more than one category. We have presented each tip in only one category. The category most likely to overlap with others deals with security and ethics. No matter your area of interest for the book, we strongly encourage you to review that section carefully.

Hardware and Equipment

Lawyers often ask our opinions about what hardware will work best for them in their offices and sometimes out of their offices. We regularly check out new hardware so that we can write and talk about it. We do not suggest that we have checked out every piece of hardware that has come on the market; we have not tried to do that, as the task would prove insurmountable.

Through our efforts, however, we have found hardware that we think works well and can prove useful to lawyers and have identified some of that hardware for you in the tips included in this book and in our other articles and programs.

We do not suggest that there are no other pieces of hardware that may work as well for you as those we discuss, nor do we suggest that you may not prefer different hardware more for your practice. Sometimes beauty does lie in the beholder's eye. What we talk about in this section works for us and impressed us as useful for lawyers. Even if you do not decide to get the hardware we talk about in this section, we think you will find the section useful. If nothing else, it should give you a place to start looking and something to use as a standard for the comparison of hardware in which you may be interested.

Please remember that hardware manufacturers survive on making new products and offering them for sale. Sometimes a manufacturer makes substantial and substantive changes in the newer models; sometimes the new model makes only some cosmetic changes. Sometimes the newer model does not work as well or reliably as its predecessor. Accordingly, you should not assume that just because the manufacturer offers a newer model of the hardware we talk about that the newer model will work better. You should also take note of the fact that when a new model comes out, you can often pick up the older model at a substantial discount that more than makes up for the additional features offered with the new model. Be a smart buyer; in deciding whether to pay the cost of the new model to get the additional features or take the discount and get the older model, compare the features of the new model to the older one and then look at the price differential. If the new features do not help you, then you do not need them. If the cost of the new features does not appear to justify what they add, you are well advised to get the older model and save the money. On the other hand, if the new features make the product significantly better, they may justify their cost.

If you do not get a substantial discount for the discontinued model and the new model appears at least as good as the discontinued one, then you will likely do better getting the new model.

Carry a Cellular Hotspot

Public Wi-Fi connections expose you to greater risk than secure private connections. You can limit your exposure and maintain contact in most cases by carrying your own secure cellular-based hotspot. Most carriers offer these devices as stand-alones. Many smartphones and tablets can also double as hotspots in a pinch. We recommend going with the stand-alone devices as they generally work faster, have their own battery power (usually longer lasting than the smartphone batteries), and do not drain power from your phone. They often offer the flexibility of allowing a larger number of connections as well. At the present time, these devices (sometimes referred to generically as "Mi-Fi") generally have the following characteristics:

1. They allow multiple connections, often up to 15.
2. They work with all Wi-Fi–enabled devices on all platforms.
3. They cost around $50 or less with service-plan subscriptions.
4. You can include it in your bundled device (shared access) plan with major carriers.
5. Run at 4G speeds (when available).
6. Have password-protected secure access.
7. You can get versions for all major carriers.
8. Some contain memory for storage and data sharing as well.

E-readers versus Tablets

While most tablets and many smartphones can double as e-reader devices using available apps (most notably Kindle and Nook apps or iBooks on iOS devices), we have some good reasons for also getting dedicated e-readers. The two best-known and most successful players in the e-reader industry, Amazon (Kindle devices) and Barnes & Noble (Nook devices) have tried to challenge the tablet market by offering color display tablet devices capable of streaming media as well as presenting books. The tablet devices offered by Amazon do not compare favorably to the leading Android-based tablets (Samsung's offerings) or the iPad in terms of their functionality. They do compare favorably in terms of cost. If you simply want a device that will let you stream media, play movies, read books and magazines, and let you play a few games and answer some e-mails, these tablets may prove to be a viable option for you. If you want more, you will not match the functionality of the Samsung tablets, let alone the even more functional iPad from Apple. The newest tablets from Barnes & Noble are, in fact, Samsung tablets put out under the Nook name and are far more functional than the older Nook tablets.

Amazon and Barnes & Noble, along with several other vendors, offer a gray-scale e-ink technology in smaller and less expensive devices. These devices do not compete, in terms of watching videos, browsing the Internet, or streaming media, with your iPad or Samsung tablet but supplement it in two very important ways. First, their more diminutive size makes them an easier carry, and second, their display technology makes them usable in direct sunlight (which color tablets generally are not). We regularly use iPads and e-readers (we prefer the Kindle Voyage of the currently available e-ink books). You can check out the various models, features, and pricing structures at the Amazon and Barnes & Noble websites (www.amazon .com) (www.barnesandnoble.com).

Laser Multifunction Printers

When you are starting out, or when your printer/copier/fax/scanner breaks at the wrong time, it can be tempting to look for the least expensive option to replace it with until you can invest the time and money it takes to purchase a quality product. Most lawyers agree with the utility of a multifunction printer/copier/scanner/fax machine. It saves on real estate in your office and frees up your computer ports for other useful devices. The question that often arises is whether you should buy an inkjet multifunction or a laser multifunction printer. We suggest you go with laser. The cost savings over the lifetime of the device will more than account for the up-front costs. Not to mention the headaches you will save yourself over running to the store to buy toner.

Laser multifunction printers are more expensive, and the toner for a laser printer is also more expensive. However, the cost-per-page of owning an inkjet is higher, they tend to print slower, and overall they tend to be messier than their laser counterparts. Given these disadvantages, we overwhelmingly recommend you use a laser multifunction device. An example of a laser multifunction printer that one of the authors recommends is the Samsung Multifunction Xpress C1860-FW. At 16.5" x 16.8" x 17.6", it should fit comfortably on a surface inside your office.

Cover Your Keyboard

The keyboard is one of the most exposed areas of your laptop or tablet, and damaging it can render your device useless. There are a variety of ways you can damage your keyboard. The keys can wear down, the wires connecting the keys can wear out or become non-responsive, and almost every key leaves enough of a gap to catch crumbs or dust that interferes with its use. Not to mention the dreaded risk of spilling liquids on it. The best way to protect your keyboard is to abstain from exposing it to liquids and food that may seep under the keys. Unfortunately, we often spend too much time around keyboards to avoid consuming liquids and food around them. Keyboards are easily protected from these elements, though, and a prime example that an ounce of prevention can be worth a pound of cure.

Keyboard covers, like the KB Cover, come in a variety of shapes and sizes to fit snugly and comfortably over your device. The covers may be see-through, allowing you to view your keys, or they may identify the key with their own style (larger font, higher contrast, etc.). When choosing your keyboard cover, you will want to look for a thickness that balances durability with good keyboard feedback. Too stiff and it may not register the key that you are inputting. Both silicone and thermoplastic urethane are popular choices.

As an added bonus, keyboard covers are easier to keep clean. Some studies indicate your keyboard can carry more germs than a bathroom toilet. Most keyboard covers can easily lift off of the keys and be run under some water for a quick scrub. If you do take your cover off and clean it, you should let it dry thoroughly before placing it back on your keys.

Bose Soundlink III

- GREAT sound
- Bluetooth wireless (pair and play)
- Portable (less than 3 lb.)
- Auxiliary input for non-Bluetooth connectivity
- USB input for software updates
- Rechargeable lithium-ion battery
- Up to 14 hours of playback from rechargeable batteries (lithium-ion)
- $299.95 www.bose.com

Bose has a reputation for providing outstanding sound equipment. They offer a wide selection of wired and wireless speakers, headsets, earbuds, and other audio enhancement devices. The Soundlink III gives you rich sound that will enable you and your friends to enjoy your music on the go. It connects using a standard audio cable or wirelessly using Bluetooth. Although the Soundlink is in its third generation, you can still find the earlier devices (Soundlink and Soundlink II) for sale in various stores (Costco currently discounts the Soundlink II). The earlier iterations are only marginally different in quality and sound from the current generation; so if you have an earlier version, there is little justification for upgrading. If you can get a good price on an earlier version, there is no reason not to grab it. If you really work at it, you might detect some sound-quality differences, but they are pretty comparable.

Bose Soundlink Mini II

- Surprisingly good sound
- Bluetooth wireless (pair and play)
- Portable (1.5 lb.)
- Auxiliary input for non-Bluetooth connectivity
- Rechargeable lithium-ion battery
- Up to seven hours of playback from rechargeable batteries (lithium-ion)
- $199.95 www.bose.com

The Bose Soundlink Mini II is another great offering from the folks at Bose. Small, very portable, and designed for travel, the Soundlink Mini II gives you sound much richer than its size would suggest. It connects using a standard audio cable or wirelessly using Bluetooth. We don't want to sound like the Bose PR team and we have no stock in the company, but we surely do enjoy its products. They are a bit pricey, but sometimes you get what you pay for. The Mini II is a recent release and the primary difference between it and the Mini is the ability to use it as a speakerphone. If you are willing to live without that feature, you can still find the Mini at places like Costco at substantial discounts.

By the way, Bose makes this in almost any color you want, as long as you want silver. Bose does sell protective cases with trim in five colors to give you the ability to personalize.

Bose Noise-Canceling Headphones

- Something new from the king of the hill
- In-ear (QC20) Quiet Comfort acoustic noise-canceling headphones—the first in-ear noise-canceling headphones ever offered by Bose
- One of the best noise-cancellation systems available; capable of making the roar of a giant passenger jet fade into the background
- Aware Mode lets you hear what is going on around you, if you want to (just push a control button to turn the feature on and off)
- $299.95 www.bose.com

The QC20 is the newest and smallest noise-cancellation device from Bose. Typical of Bose-engineered sound systems, the QC20 generates very high-quality sound. We have tried a lot of in-ear noise-cancellation devices from a variety of manufacturers and like these the best. They are small, lightweight, easily packable, well designed, and produce gangbuster sound.

Set Up a Functional Storage Plan

Setting up a functional storage plan for your office means getting sufficient hardware (hard disks, Wi-Fi, routers, etc.) to store the data and provide reasonable backup, and creating an organizational structure that you and your staff can work with comfortably. Many lawyers (particularly those who have been in practice for a while) find that they are most comfortable with a simple structure that mimics electronically the paper system they grew up with as young lawyers. That means, effectively, that you have a folder for each client (think of it as a file drawer). In that drawer you have a folder for each matter for that client. In each client matter you have a separate folder for each of several basic categories of documents. For example, in a litigation matter, you might have a file for correspondence, client documents, pleadings, discovery, motions, etc. Different matters will have different folder structures.

Label documents so that you can easily find them. A sample structure may look like this: "15-0106 Smith-Jones negotiations." That translates into a letter dated January 6, 2015, from Smith to Jones respecting negotiations. Another example for a pleading may look like this: "15-0106 Amended Complaint"—simply put, the date and type of document. Used consistently, this approach has the advantage of automatically storing the documents in chronological order in your computer.

Seagate Wireless Plus Mobile Storage

If you find yourself traveling someplace with limited wireless access and need access to a hefty amount of files, you may want to check out the Seagate Wireless Plus Mobile Storage device. The Wireless Plus provides up to 2 TB of storage space, 10-plus hours of battery life, and a built-in Wi-Fi network that will support up to eight devices, all in one device that is about the same size as a regular USB 3.0 portable drive. Once connected to the storage device, you can stream digital content from it using a mobile App or network browser. This is all particularly handy if you rely on a tablet device.

With the iPad, for instance, one of the biggest shortcomings is the limited memory available and the inability to transfer data to or from the iPad by a USB connection (for any who have not seen an iPad, it lacks a USB port). The Seagate Wireless Plus Mobile Storage offers a solution to this dilemma. For around $200, you can expand your iPad, increasing storage to 2 TB of storage. The drive will also synchronize with Dropbox and Google Drive, bringing the cloud along with you.

Hover Cam Mini 5

- Hi-Res 5 MP autofocus camera
- Scanner, camera, presenter, webcam (works with Skype)
- Use cable or plug into laptop USB connector
- Autofocus
- Folds into a very small package
- $299.99 www.thehovercam.com

This is one of the slickest little devices going for litigators, educators, or anyone who does presentations. One of the devices you want as a presenter is a document camera to enable you to project an image of a document that you did not obtain in an electronic format and do not have time to scan. It also gives you the ability to do real-time markups on a copy of the document and project those as well. Simply put, if you present electronically, a document camera is one of the tools you absolutely want to have available to you.

In today's world, we prize mobility and portability. This little gem folds up and travels virtually invisibly in a jacket pocket, or easily in a purse or briefcase. You can use it with a desktop, but it works best with a laptop. You plug it into a USB port on the computer and connect the computer to a projector and you have the ability to show the image on the display and/or project it on a screen. Cleverly enough, this also works as a webcam should you have a laptop that lacks one.

If you want a more powerful camera, check out the somewhat larger (but still fairly small) 8 megapixel 30 fps Solo 8 from the same company.

Visit the Colonel! (No, Not the Chicken Guy)

- High-quality leather goods
- Phone and tablet cases
- Briefcases
- Excellent choice for gifts
- A nice present for yourself
- Well made
- Very protective of your electronics devices

Colonel Littleton is certainly not the only purveyor of good-quality leather cases for electronic devices. The Colonel, however, enjoys a reputation for producing high-quality, durable leather products at reasonable prices. Just to give you an example, I bought one of the No. 5 pockets for my iPad several years ago and have used it constantly. It is now carrying its fourth iPad and going strong! The Colonel does not use thin, fragile leathers; he uses thick, strong, durable leather pieces that provide protection for your devices and look good while doing it.

Get a Tablet

For many people, a tablet will suffice, and they do not need a full computer (laptop or desktop). For some people it will not, and they need both. Whichever category you fall in, having a tablet can make things easier for you, and we recommend you get one. If you want a tablet, we think the iPad represents the best option for most people.

Why get a tablet? Tablets weigh less, take up less space, cost less, have longer battery life, and travel better than laptops. Moreover, they do almost everything a laptop can do for you (some software does not exist in tablet mode, and some software does not function as well on a tablet).

If your primary goals focus on e-mail, web surfing, communications, reviewing documents, and entertainment (game playing and media streaming), a tablet should suffice for your needs. If you want to do document creation and heavy editing of documents, we recommend you use a computer. Even if you get a computer, having the tablet means you do not need to schlep the computer everywhere. We expect that you will find that most of the time you can just carry the tablet and will use your laptop less and less as you get used to using the tablet.

If you practice law, particularly litigation, you will probably want both a tablet and a laptop, as they can serve different functions for you in court.

If you want a tablet, we like the iPad and the Samsung Galaxy. While the Galaxy has very good specifications and is quite well made, we prefer the iPad, largely due to the fact that the iTunes App Store, the source for most apps for the iPad, has a larger and more varied selection of apps in all categories than the Android App stores, such as Google Play, that service the Android devices, such as the Galaxy.

Take Your iPad to Court

The iPad is a useful tool in the courtroom. It really comes in handy when it comes to opening statements, closing arguments, and, on occasion, oral arguments of motions. If you dislike holding yellow tablets or notebooks with notes during an opening statement or a closing argument, you may find the iPad to be an excellent substitute for a multitude of reasons. The iPad's size and configuration let you carry and hold it more easily. It also presents a more finished and professional appearance to the jury.

You can keep your notes in any one of many format choices, whichever you prefer. You can set them up in a word processing App such as Word or Pages, or use an outliner App like Omni Outliner. The authors prefer the outliners to word processors, but it is a subjective preference. There are even several mind-mapping apps you can try, including Mindjet, MindNode, MindMeister, and iThoughts.

You can also use the iPad to control presentations, with Keynote Remote or i-Clickr PowerPoint Remote. With Keynote Remote you can control your presentation and still view your presenter notes without sharing them with the viewers.

Portable Hard Drives

- Available in USB 2.0 and USB 3.0 versions (3.0 is backward-compatible with 2.0)
- Very reasonably priced (regularly on sale online and at Costco in the range of $100 for a 2 TB drive)
- Work with Mac OS and Windows OS systems (interchangeably if formatted for Windows)
- Excellent choice for backup of a laptop computer
- Excellent choice for additional memory for programs and files
- Many manufacturers including Buffalo, WD (Western Digital), Seagate, Toshiba, and La Cie, among many others
- We have found WD and Seagate drives particularly reliable and reasonably priced as a general rule
- Newest drives use flash memory, making them smaller, faster, and less prone to failure (but still more expensive)

Hard drives tend to cause most computer failures; whether it is a hardware failure or the corruption of system files on the drive, it can effectively disable a computer. You can help protect your practice from the impact of such a problem (particularly if it occurs during the middle of a trial) by cloning a bootable hard drive (before failure) and bringing that portable drive with you. You can then use the clone as the controlling drive for the computer if the onboard drive fails. You can get to substantially the same place by simply creating a bootable drive and adding the required programs and data.

Logitech Ultrathin Keyboard iPad Cover

While many of us happily use the virtual keyboards built into the operating systems for our iPad devices, some of us prefer a physical keyboard, at least some of the time. If you plan to do any serious typing, we recommend that you consider a Bluetooth keyboard for the iPad, as it seems to make it easier and allow you to type more rapidly than using the virtual keyboard. We have lost track of the number of manufacturers of Bluetooth wireless keyboards that will pair with the iPad and the iPad Mini devices. We are, however, particularly partial to some of the Logitech products. Logitech has been around for a while and has a reputation for making good, reliable computer accessories. It has carried that reputation into the tablet category as well, making Bluetooth-enabled keyboards designed to use with tablets. Recognizing that many users will also want to protect the display on their tablet, Logitech has created a number of covers and folders that combine a physical Bluetooth-enabled keyboard with protection for the tablet's display. One of our favorites is the Ultrathin Magnetic clip-on keyboard cover available for the iPad Air (list price $99.99) and for the iPad Mini/Mini with Retina Display (list price $89.99). They have the same design and functionality but differ in size to match the device for which they were created. They both have rechargeable batteries that can last for several months between charges. They both function as covers that hinge to magnetic connectors that you connect to the iPad, similarly to Apple's own Smart Cover. They both provide a multi-angled stand for your iPad to make it easier for you to see while typing. Oh yeah, they are both very nice keyboards that work very well (note that the keyboard for the iPad Air is approximately full size and the keyboard for the Mini is a bit smaller, reflective of the reduced size of the cover to fit the smaller tablet).

Mophie Juice Packs

If you find yourself regularly falling into a battery slump for your smartphone, check out the Mophie Juice Pack. It provides extended power and protection all in one ultrathin package. The case provides rubberized support pads on the inside, protecting your phone from drops and hard falls. The 2,600mAh delivers more than 60 percent extra battery for the Juice Pack. This means that while an average iPhone 6 provides 12 hours of battery life with active Internet use, an iPhone 6 encased in the Mophie Juice Pack provides up to 22 hours of battery life with active Internet use. A notch on the back of the case allows you to turn the pack off and on, conserving energy for when you need it most.

The Juice Pack enables priority sync as well, so when you plug the cable into your phone to recharge, it charges the phone first and then moves on to charging the Juice Pack.

Mophie also offers the Juice Pack Air for the iPhone 6, which delivers 100 percent extra battery.

Present Like a Pro with a Wireless Presenter

Lawyers often make presentations, both in and out of court. Using PowerPoint or other slide programs to facilitate those presentations has become almost second nature to lawyers. When making a presentation, there are real advantages to mobility. Tying yourself to a computer to manually change slides can detract from your presentation. Having a wireless remote control device allows you freedom of motion and building a laser pointer into it gives you the ability to emphasize particular points visually as well as verbally. We have found many wireless controllers, all of which will provide some or all of those benefits. The first part of this tip is that you find one, get it, and use it. The second part is that we are very partial to two from Logitech and we recommend that you look seriously at these two devices. Both are very easy to learn and use and have plug and play compatibility. If you look on the Logitech website, they show the devices as Windows compatible, without mentioning the Mac. We have used them successfully with both Macs and Windows, however.

The R400 uses 2.4GHz wireless technology to provide you with about 50 feet of range and has a built-in class-2 red laser pointer. It lists for $49.99.

The R800 gives you a 100-foot range, a green laser pointer (green lasers are more powerful than red lasers), and an LCD display to help you keep track of your time, battery power, and wireless reception.

Get a Mac!

For many years the built-for-Windows computer ruled the roost in the law office. In recent years, more and more lawyers, particularly those in solo and small firm practices, have adopted the Mac instead of built-for-Windows computers. The trend really picked up as a result of the popularity of Apple's iPod, iPhone, and iPad devices introducing people to Apple hardware and operating systems. Ultimately, more and more lawyers discovered that, although Apple hardware may cost a bit more to acquire, in the long run it generally costs less in terms of frustration, aggravation, and, yes, money, to run on a Mac system. Some of the reasons for this include:

1. The Mac OS X has proved very stable and upgrading from one version to another usually works easily.
2. Apple builds exceptionally good and very reliable hardware.
3. Apple's control over both the hardware and the operating system allows Apple to design the hardware and operating system to work well together and take advantage of each other's features.
4. Apple devices and operating systems are more user friendly than the competition.
5. You can run a Mac-based office without an IT department.
6. If you really need to run a Windows program, you can run Windows on the Mac using Bootcamp, Fusion, or Parallels.
7. Now that more vendors have moved to cloud-based service systems, the issue of proprietary software not working with the Mac OS is becoming moot.

Adonit Jot Fine Point Stylus

Stylus tools are handy if you prefer the pen-and-paper method of note taking but want the functionality of electronic notes. For some, the simple act of writing notes is part of their creative process, but how many times have you misplaced the legal pad, or maybe paper napkin, on which you wrote your most brilliant thought? To avoid that, you should try using a stylus with your iPad or tablet to take notes or brainstorm when the thought hits you.

In the early years of touch screens, the screens were resistive, meaning you could touch it with anything and the screen would respond. Then, all you had to do was make sure the thing you used to touch it was not so pointy it would scratch or damage the screen. In recent years screens have transitioned away from being resistive to being capacitive, relying on the conductivity of a human finger to respond. This has triggered a change in stylus tools, moving away from the traditional plastic stick to a capacitive tip.

The Adonit Jot Pro has one of the most precise tips on the market and looks a bit different than the tips you may be accustomed to seeing over the years. Most capacitive tips are round and soft, but the Jot Pro is a very hard and fine tip that more closely resembles that of a mechanical pencil. It is separated from the surface of your tablet or phone by a large, round, transparent capacitive disk on the end, preventing the tip from damaging your screen.

Grid-It

If you are a visual person, using a system like GRID-IT can help prevent you from absent-mindedly forgetting to pack an important cable or device when you go somewhere. If you don't need that help, the GRID-IT will still help you keep your electronics and attachments organized and together so that you can easily find them.

The GRID-IT is a rubberized woven elastic object-retention system to organize your gadgets. It fits neatly inside bags and briefcases to keep you organized on the go. The system holds thumb drives, spare batteries, business card cases, charging and connector cables, cameras, reading glasses—almost anything you can think of. The elastic bands hold the item firmly in place, and the rubberized backing prevents it from sliding around. If the contents you are organizing are fragile, you should still place the organizer in a padded pocket, but if the goal is solely organization of small electronic devices and cables, this system does it well.

Get a Good Scanner

There are a multitude of scanners out there; you are really only limited by the configurations, features, and prices that appeal to you. For most small offices, the multifunction device (sometimes called an "all-in-one") will represent your best investment. These devices use the same hardware to scan, copy, print, and fax. There was a time when we advocated against these because if you use one and it breaks, you are effectively out of business. However, they have become much more reliable in recent years. We like them and use them. If a breakdown concerns you, get a backup device; that is a piece of good planning, anyway.

Features to look for in a scanner:

1. Duplex scanning
2. High-capacity document feeder
3. Scan speed

If you want a small stand-alone scanner, you will have to look long and hard for a better buy than the Fujitsu Scansnap ix500. We have recommended the Scansnap line for a long time and continue to do so. The ix500 holds up to 50 sheets of paper in the automatic feeder and can handle letter- or legal-size documents, even if there are mixed sizes in the set you are scanning. This scanner scans at a rate of 25 pages per minute and can duplex scan (scan both sides of the page) in a single pass, thus including all of our favorite features in a scanner.

Build Your Own Cloud Storage: Cloudstor and Pogoplug

If you have some trepidation about storing your data on a server that could be on foreign soil, then the option exists to set up your own cloud storage. In the past, hosting your own cloud storage proved challenging and very cumbersome, but now it has become far easier to execute with Pogoplug and Buffalo's Cloudstor, a network-attached storage system. Now you can set up your own cloud-based data and store or access your data wherever you want. Pogoplug even provides an App allowing you to access your file storage similar to Dropbox and Box.

Buffalo Technology's Cloudstor uses Pogoplug technology and offers an easy and reasonably priced way to maintain your own data in the cloud. Installation and setup is fairly simple: just take the Cloudstor out of the box and plug it in, then connect the Ethernet cord to your router. Go to the computer and open a webpage and go to http://cloudstor.pogoplug.com/activate to activate the device. Once you go through the motions of activating the device, you need to set up a free Pogoplug account, which will then give you the ability to access the Cloudstor from any of your computers when they are connected to the Internet. You can access your data without any proprietary software by using a browser and logging into your account at www.buffalocloudstor.com (you can also log into your account directly at the Pogoplug site), but having the software on each of your computers puts an alias of the Cloudstor device on each desktop, making it very easy to access and use the information.

Cloudstor and Pogoplug work with Mac OS X, Windows, and Linux systems, with special software designed for each. In addition, you can get Pogoplug apps for your iOS (iPhone, iPad, iPod), Android, and Palm devices. You get the iOS App at Apple's App Store, the Android App from the Android Market, and the Palm App from the Palm App Catalog; simply download and install each as you would any other application for that device. Once it is installed, open the application from your Internet-connected device and log into your account for access to your media and stored data.

Even though you own the server and control its physical location, you should recognize the potential vulnerability of anything stored in the cloud. Accordingly, you should continue to encrypt critical and confidential data.

Build Your Own Cloud Storage: Drobo Transporter

You can still get in on the ground floor of cloud storage. No building code issues; no permit requirements; very little effort and very little cost required.

Many manufacturers offer devices that allow you to access them through the Internet and upload or download data to them from virtually anywhere you can get Internet access.

One of our favorites, Drobo, makes the Transporter. It allows you to stake your claim in the cloud, homestead it, and operate your own cloud storage facility with plug and play simplicity. You can get one Transporter or several. If you get one, you have a place to store your data in the cloud and can access it and even synchronize it among various devices. If you get more than one and connect them to the same account, they will talk to each other and back each other up, giving you geographic redundancy. You can locate them as close or as far apart as you like. We like having one in the office and one at home. Some people have set up a Transporter in a different state to create greater redundancy. It is just as easy to set one up in San Francisco and another in Seattle or Denver (or anywhere else you choose) as it is to set up one in your home and another in your office. All it takes is getting the hardware to the location, plugging it in, and connecting it to the Internet. All devices tied to the same account can access the data on the Transporters, and the linked Transporters will set up the required protocols to securely back up to each other. The basic Transporters come without memory built in and cost about $100 each. You then have to get a hard drive for each Transporter and connect it to the Transporter (plug it in). The Transporter Private Cloud has its own storage space. Both devices work the same way; the only differences are price, shape, and the inclusion of built-in storage or the need for a separate purchase.

Protect Your Mobile Displays

Because of the way we use them, mobile devices such as smartphones and tablets have a higher risk of incurring damage, particularly to the display, than computers and even laptops that travel with us. Mobile devices usually come with displays made of glass or plastic. Although many manufacturers claim that the material used for their displays has incredible strength, the fact remains that a large number of displays fracture for a variety of reasons ranging from dropping the device to dropping something on the device to a dog using it for a chew toy. Many more develop scratches as well. While nothing can guarantee that the display will not shatter or scratch, you can reduce the risk of shattering and greatly reduce the risk of scratching by protecting the display.

The first step to protecting the display is to get a screen protector. The state of the art has moved from plastic to tempered glass as it installs better and easier and appears to provide better protection. You cannot get tempered glass protectors for all mobile devices yet, but you can find it for many, if not most, smartphones. We have moved to tempered glass screen protectors for all of our smartphones. Some manufacturers offer screen protectors that provide additional functionality, such as privacy enhancement and glare reduction. If you use your mobile devices in places where others can see the screens (such as on an airplane or in a crowded air terminal), a privacy screen gives you enhanced security against information theft.

The second step to protecting a display is to get a case for the device that has a cover that flips over the display.

You have lots of choices for both display protectors and cases with display covers. Check places like BestBuy, Amazon, Fry's, and the online stores for your device (i.e., the Apple Store for iPhones). Service providers also generally carry a selection of such devices.

Oh, and the third step is to keep the device out of the mouth of your Labrador retriever (or whatever breed of dog you may have)! Proof of the fact that nothing will guarantee that the display will not crack is that Buck (the Lab) managed to crack the bottom corner of the display of an iPad that had a plastic screen protector and a case with a screen cover. The fracture ultimately spidered throughout the entire screen. The screen protector held the fractured pieces together, which at least prevented injury to the dog. The good news: Apple Care replaced the iPad for $50.

Software

Software (aka Apps) makes our computers, smartphones, and tablets do most of what they do for us. Without software, they would largely be expensive paperweights. A good selection of software will help you get the most value and functionality from your computers, smartphones, and tablets.

For smartphones and tablets, the best source of software or Apps is the store set up for distribution of such software by the developer of the hardware operating system. The two best-known and largest providers of hardware operating systems for smartphones and tablets are Google (Android) and Apple (iOS). Google has set up the Google Play Store to distribute Apps from Google and from other developers. Apple has set up an applications section in its iTunes Store for the distribution of its own Apps, as well as Apps from other developers. While developers of other operating systems have established their own software App venue, none of the others compares favorably with the Google Play Store, and the Google Play Store is not as well developed as Apple's iTunes App Store in terms of the range or quantity of available Apps. Apple also does a better job of vetting Apps to avoid malware.

When dealing with smartphones and tablets, it is often difficult to add software to the device except through purchase at the appropriate distribution center (iTunes App Store or Google Play Store). You have an additional advantage in getting software from the operating system developer's software store in that they (particularly Apple) do some checking out of the software prior to adding it to the store, so you get a bit of protection that way.

While computer software sales have started to morph toward the same model as the Apps for smartphones and tablets, they have not yet arrived at that destination. Accordingly, you can still get lots of software directly from the publisher and easily install it on your computer. If you have opted for Apple's Macintosh OS, you can go to the Apple App Store to get software for your computer. Microsoft is moving in the same direction, including many Apps for Windows in the Microsoft Store. Acquisition of third-party software from the publisher or other vendors remains available, and installation generally poses no serious problems.

Many vendors have started offering software on a subscription basis, often called software as a service (SaaS). This approach has the advantage of giving you updates at no extra cost and with no significant effort. Some of the subscription software downloads to your computer, allowing you to run it locally and without an Internet connection. The remainder works only when you have an Internet connection. You can use the software through a browser anywhere you have Internet access, but you generally cannot use the software without the Internet.

In this section we will identify some of the software and Apps that we have found useful for computers, smartphones, and tablets. Many of the programs will give you the opportunity to try them out for a period of time or provide a limited-use version for you to try at no cost. We encourage you to take advantage of that opportunity to see the features of the program so that you can determine whether it will work well for you.

Adobe Acrobat

Adobe Acrobat long ago established itself as software that we believe belongs in every law office. The current version is Acrobat DC, which now sells as a subscription-based SaaS. Attorneys and their support staff should learn to use the features of the program and use it on a regular basis for controlling documents and exhibits and for production of documents in the course of discovery as well as in sending documents to others for collaboration. Although Acrobat comes in several versions, we recommend that law offices standardize on the Professional version on both the Macintosh OS (where no other version exists) and the Windows OS, (which has other versions) as it has features that benefit attorneys, such as true redaction capabilities.

You can find a detailed feature comparison among the leading versions of Acrobat DC at https://acrobat.adobe.com/us/en/pricing/pricing-compare-versions.html. As we write this book, Adobe is in the process of converting its software sales to a software subscription program.

While some of you may object to the concept of SaaS or subscription-based charging, it has some advantages, including that you automatically get all upgrades while your subscription is active; you get access to the online services offered by Adobe to work with the program, and you can work with PDF files in a browser and from mobile devices. The subscription is cross-platform, so you can use it when jumping from one device to another.

Firm Central

Thomson Reuters (TR), a GPSolo Division sponsor, has developed a multi-platform practice-management tool, Firm Central, to help level the playing field for solo and small-firm lawyers. If you are a WestlawNext user, your practice will get a boost from Firm Central. The software as a service joins a growing market of cloud-based practice-management tools, which promise anytime/anywhere access for lawyers no matter the size of your firm. Because it lives in the cloud, it works on both the Mac OS X and the Windows platforms. You can even access it on your iPad or tablet. Properly used, this means every client document, case law, and time and expense entry is captured and available in one easily retrievable place.

Firm Central was designed to be exactly what it is called—the hub, or center, of your firm. Not only can you handle the business of practicing law here, but you can conduct your research, gather knowledge, and better manage it to share with your team members. The addition of time and billing to the powerhouse software completes the picture.

Firm Central integrates well with several useful tools that support your practice, including the following:

- matter and document organization
- unique integration
- global search
- time and billing management
- client portal
- calendar
- deadline assistant
- enhanced mobility

The client portal was a nice addition to the software since it originally rolled out. With this feature you can invite clients to collaborate and share information in a secure environment. The portal allows you to share messages, documents, forms, and other case details with your clients.

The authors recommend that if you are going to use a public cloud, use it to run applications and store non-privileged data, or non-protected health information if applicable. Use a semiprivate cloud that you have properly vetted from a well-established and reliable provider familiar with the needs of law firms, such as Thompson Reuters, and/or a properly protected private cloud for files with your personal, privileged, or protected information. By way of example, Thomson Reuters's Firm Central employs several layers of security to protect your data, including the following:

- AES 256-bit encryption to encrypt the data stored on your servers
- 2048-bit SSL Certificates for data in transit
- secured data centers with physical and geographic redundancy
- nightly backups of data stored on servers
- highly restricted internal employee access to customer-stored data
- a viable procedure for switching from one server to another in the event of a problem with the primary server

The authors have toured the data facility utilized by West for its Firm Central operation and took due notice of the restrictive access and impressive backup measures employed by West at that facility.

Mozilla Firefox

Up until recently, Google Chrome held the lead as the preferred Web browser, especially for Windows users. Since its launch in 2008, the no-frills Web browser led the market with superior rendering speed. However, Chrome has a habit of opening multiple instances of the application, even if you have only one tab in your browser, thereby slowing down your system. In 2014, Mozilla surpassed Chrome with the launch of Firefox 31, which showcased a major interface redesign along with the huge strides the company made in reducing memory consumption and increasing startup speed.

These improvements, along with the customization opportunities, make Firefox a popular choice for your default Web browser. Mozilla Firefox excels at customizability, with its extensive database of extensions and themes. Extensions are program features you can add to your Web browser to enhance your browsing experience. Themes are more decorative but can be designed to arrange the user interface in a way that you will likely find more useful and intuitive. A relatively simple interface is the foundation of Mozilla Firefox. Once you install the Web browser, you can choose to add as much or as little as you desire. Firefox works very well on both the Windows and Mac platforms. We have found that some programs do not play well with Safari on the Mac but work just fine with Firefox; so even if you use Mac and prefer Safari as your primary browser, you should download and install a copy of Firefox.

Mind Maps

Although some people may think that a mind map refers to the location in the brain where certain processes take place, and others may think it provides directions for brain surgeons to locate parts of the brain, mind mapping offers very different insight.

Mind mapping allows you to develop a concept or think something through by displaying relationships to each other. It offers something akin to outlining, but at a much more graphic level. If you learn or work better visually, you need to try mind mapping.

Those of you who do not take the time to outline oral and written arguments would probably benefit from doing that. You might benefit even more from preparing a mind map first, developing and refining that into a more finished product, and then using the mind map to assist you in developing the outline. You can then work off the outline to make the oral presentation and/or write the argument.

While you can do a mind map using pen and paper, you will probably find it easier to do on a computer or a tablet. You could create a mind map successfully using a basic drawing App on your computer or tablet, but several companies have developed software to make the task even easier to accomplish. Several of the Apps have trial modes available to let you try before you buy. The price range on the mind-mapping Apps goes from very inexpensive to somewhat more costly, but we have not yet found one that we thought prohibitively or even unfairly expensive. Some of our favorites include NovaMind, Mindjet, and ConceptDraw. One of the least expensive and well-designed programs we have found, Inspiration, was designed for the educational market, but works for others.

Electronic Trial Notebooks

Trial books are a useful guide and tool for any litigator. Creating a trial book will help ensure that you are ready for trial. Regardless of whether you use a physical trial book or a digital one at trial, we think you should start with a digital one when you are putting it together. There are several ways you can create trial books, but the two the authors favor are Microsoft OneNote for Windows or Circus Ponies NoteBook for Mac users. Both allow you to easily incorporate text, PDF and images into your notebook. You can set up tabs in your digital notebook to further organize your thoughts.

Some of the perks of using digital trial books include the following:

- easier to navigate with search features
- much easier to carry around
- environmentally friendly with less paper usage
- automatic real-time saving to preserve your ideas

Microsoft OneNote has a template of trial notebook available for users with OneNote 2007 or later. When you open the program, it is structured to appear similar to a three-ring binder, with tabs across the top and pages broken out along the side. You can further group sub-pages and pages. Conveniently, your notes will sync to any One-Note App you have installed on a device (laptop, iPad, tablet, etc.).

Circus Ponies NoteBook works with both Mac OS and the iPad. It has a very strong outliner feature. You can expand and collapse portions of your outlines to show varying amounts of detail. This product features a unique multi-font text editor as well. You can add attachments to your notes for fast reference. Each item that you enter or place in your outline encodes unique attributes revealing when it was created, when it was last changed, any keywords assigned to it, and icons or "stickers" attached to it. These attributes can be made visible or hidden. Please note that the Circus Ponies company has apparently closed its doors recently as it has taken its site down and you cannot buy its Apps on the Apple sites. If you have it, it still works. If not, you can no longer easily get it. Microsoft now offers OneNote for the iPad and the Mac. We are searching for a viable replacement to Circus Ponies.

Some Common Microsoft Shortcuts

Since time is a lawyer's stock and trade, saving a few seconds here and there can add up to substantial dollars over time. These common Microsoft Office shortcuts can help you shave those seconds off the time it takes to draft documents:

TABLE 1
Common Microsoft Shortcuts

Ctrl+S saves your current work.

Ctrl+O opens a new document.

Ctrl+Z and Alt-Backspace undo the last thing you did.

Ctrl+Y undoes the last undo (or redoes).

Ctrl+A selects everything in the open window, whether it's all the files in a folder or the entire document.

Ctrl+H deletes the selection.

Ctrl+C copies the selection.

Ctrl+V pastes the clipboard contents.

Ctrl+F and F3 launch the program's search or find tool.

Ctrl+Home moves the cursor to the beginning of the open file or document.

Ctrl+End moves the cursor to the end of the open file or document.

Alt+Tab switches between open Apps.

Windows logo key+L will lock the computer.

Ctrl+plus (+) or Ctrl+minus (-) will zoom in or out of your screen.

TABLE 2
Microsoft Windows Mail Shortcuts

Ctrl+R to reply to a message.

Ctrl+Shift+R to reply all.

Ctrl+F to forward a message.

Ctrl+M to move an item to a different folder.

Ctrl+J to toggle between marking a message as junk or not junk.

Ctrl+Shift+U will show only unread messages.

Ctrl+Shift+A will show all messages.

Ctrl+U to mark a message as unread.

Ctrl+Q to mark a message as read.

Ctrl+N to create a new message.

Doodle

An online scheduling tool that makes scheduling meetings with multiple parties easier. You can poll potential attendees with a selection of dates and times to identify when maximum attendance will be possible. The site walks you through the process in four simple steps:

1. Create an event.
2. Propose a range of times and dates.
3. Choose your poll settings.
4. Invite participants to your poll.

Creating an event is simple: Fill out the Doodle form with the title, location, and description of the event. This information will be conveyed to your poll participants. Enter your name as administrator, along with your e-mail address, to receive a link to view, update, or edit the poll.

At the next step, proposing dates and times, you can select several dates and time ranges. These can be nonconsecutive dates and times. If you are scheduling a Web or teleconference, and your potential attendees are in multiple time zones, the authors recommend that you enable Time-Zone Support in order to avoid time zone conversion confusion.

Your poll settings can be adjusted to suit your needs. For example, you can make this a Yes/No poll ("Yes, I can make this time" or "No, that time is not good for me") or make it a Yes/No/If Need Be poll, in which users can identify times that they are available but do not prefer. You can hide the poll from other participants in order to keep each potential attendee's schedule and availability confidential from the other poll participants. If you are interested in controlling the size of each meeting, you can limit the number of participants per option. Using this feature will remove an option once the designated number of participants has selected it.

You can invite participants to your poll via e-mail, Facebook, or Twitter. You can link your e-mail account with your doodle account to import addresses for participants you intend to invite.

The basic scheduling Doodle service is free, with unlimited polls and participants available. You can add features such as ad-free experience or SSL encryption by upgrading to Doodle Premium, but the authors find this to be an unnecessary measure.

Google Scholar

Google Scholar offers a free legal research tool that may be a good starting point for any attorney. In 2009, Google announced its intentions to add legal opinions to its Google Scholar database. The service aims to provide full legal opinions from both state and federal courts, with the opinions being fully searchable through the Google Scholar search engine. The case law is set up similarly to Westlaw and Lexis-Nexis. For instance, case citations within an opinion link to the case being referenced. Google Scholar uses a tab labeled "How cited" to link the reader to other cases from state and federal appellate courts that have cited the case being reviewed. It also links to any citations in scholarly documents that have been indexed by Google Scholar.

To get started, pull up scholar.google.com and, under the search box, select Case law. This leads you to the option of choosing a jurisdiction; you can limit your search results to federal courts or a specific state court.

Google Scholar does not offer a means to Shepardize a case. While the "How cited" tab will pull up case law in which it was cited, there is no reference to how the case was treated to help you determine if it is still good law. You would have to read every case in which it was cited to determine the status of the precedence. In the end, there are several pros and cons to Google Scholar, but as far as free tools go, it is not a bad one to keep handy.

CodeTwo Outlook Attachment Reminder

Ever send an e-mail with an attachment, but forget to actually attach the attachment? The world of computer users consists of two groups: those who have forgotten an attachment and those who will forget an attachment. The bad news is that for those who forgot it, there is nothing we can do for you. What is done is done. The good news is that we have a solution for those of you who have not yet forgotten an attachment. The better news is that those who have made the mistake in the past can still use this tip!

CodeTwo develops software to benefit Microsoft Outlook and Exchange users. One of the useful tools they developed is the Outlook Attachment Reminder, an add-on that prompts you if you hit send on an e-mail and forgot an attachment. The add-on identifies e-mails missing attachments by scanning the e-mail for words such as "attached" or "enclosed." If your e-mail includes one of these words, or a variation of the word, and does not have an attachment, the add-on generates a prompt inquiring whether you forgot an attachment. If yes, you can go back to your e-mail and attach; if no, simply select "No" and the message will continue on its way.

To install the add-on, simply go to www.codetwo.com, download the installer, and launch it on your computer. You should make sure Outlook is closed prior to installing the program. Once you have the program installed on your machine, the add-on is ready to scan your outgoing Outlook e-mail and alert you whenever there are missing attachments.

ConceptDraw Office 3

ConceptDraw Office 3 provides an excellent suite of programs for lawyers seeking to organize their cases and their practices. Although not designed specifically for lawyers, it works as well as or better than many programs specifically built for law office use. Current pricing for the suite is $499. If you don't want the entire package, you can purchase the three component programs for $199 each. You can try each program prior to buying it, and it works on Mac OS and Windows.

The suite includes:

ConceptDraw Pro 10. ConceptDraw provides drawing tools to assist you in organizing and displaying information visually. It offers the ability to create drawings, timelines, flow charts, and other visual presentations. The company offers a solution pack with an ever-growing number of preset solutions, as well as object libraries and templates. You can export your product to PowerPoint and many other programs using standard graphic image formats. The solution pack includes models ranging from infographics to Venn diagrams.

ConceptDraw Mindmap 8. Mindmap 8 offers one of the easier-to-use mind-mapping programs but still brings a lot of sophistication and versatility to the party. If you are a visual thinker, you should definitely try mind mapping as a way to organize thoughts and presentations. You can start from scratch or use one of the structures available in the library as your starting point. You can transfer information from Microsoft Office files and output into presentations.

ConceptDraw PROJECT 7. Project 7 offers a project-management solution. It gives you an easy way to set up a structure for the handling of a project in your office and keep track of its evolution. One of its more impressive features, the dashboard, hides much of the data and gives you a clean visual perspective showing the current status of the project.

DEVONthink

Devon Technologies has created a very useful and functional document management system for the Mac OS (sorry, there is no Windows version). They offer three levels of the program: a personal version for $49.95, a professional version for $79.95, and DEVONthink Pro Office for $149.95. For the reasons we will discuss, we particularly recommend that you use the Pro Office version, even if you practice as a solo. Devon has adopted a smart approach to licensing; they license the person and not the computer, so you can use your copy on multiple computers, but others in your office who will use the program need their own copy. You can get a time-limited demo version of the software to try it out and see if you like it. If you decide to stay with it, you can convert that to a full program by purchasing and installing a license key.

You can go to the company's website at www.devontechnologies.com to get a detailed feature comparison of the three versions and also find out about other supporting programs the company makes available. We prefer the Pro Office version to the other versions, as its feature set includes all the features of the lesser versions plus support for scanning and OCR (including Scansnap support), e-mail archiving, and Web sharing. The lesser programs do not include those features, and we think that the scanning/OCR support alone is worth the price of admission.

Some of the things DEVONthink will do for you include keeping case files, document files, notes, e-mails, and other documents in order for you. If you work on the Mac platform and want to move to a practice environment that depends less on paper and more on electronic files, we have not found a better document management program for the Mac.

CLIO

"Money makes the world go round."

For those of you who enjoy Broadway musicals, we chose to start this very practical tip with a line from a song from the musical *Cabaret*. For those not into musicals, the point still stands. A law office survives because it bills time and recovers payment for the efforts expended on behalf of clients. Lawyers who do not keep regular time records generally lose a considerable amount of their billings and, correspondingly, their income. Lawyers who bill on an hourly basis need to recognize a basic rule of law office business: "Clients almost never pay for time unless you bill them for it."

One of the most essential pieces of law office software then becomes a time and billing program. To function well, it has to work, be easy to use, and be easy to access. Some of the reasons we particularly like CLIO:

1. It works on multiple platforms.
2. As it is cloud-based, you can access it anywhere and from any device with an Internet connection.
3. It is easy to use.
4. It handles both your operating and your trust accounts interactively and smoothly.
5. It simply works!

Note that CLIO has other features available, including contacts management, calendaring, and documents management. Those features function competently, but there are other solutions that do them as well or better, in our opinion. We don't care. CLIO's claim to fame and to your computer real estate is billing. For a small firm or solo practice, we have not found anything we like better. If you use a Mac, we have found nothing we think can come close to it.

We can record time, expenses, and payments, or generate bills from anyplace in the world and send them by e-mail to our clients or to the office where they can be printed and snail-mailed. CLIO provides its services on a subscription basis, starting at $39 per user per month (based on annual billing) (www.goclio.com).

Microsoft Office 365

Everyone knows or should know about Microsoft Office. It comes in a few different structures that include different programs, but the big four that serve as the basic core of the suite are Word, Power-Point, Outlook, and Excel. Most law offices use Microsoft Office, or at least a part of it in their practice. Microsoft has created robust Mac iterations of Office with the almost completely perfect ability to move files from a Mac to the Windows platform and conversely. (There are still occasional hiccups due to some formatting differences, but the files transfer and can be corrected easily when necessary.)

Recently, Microsoft ventured into the SaaS arena with Microsoft Office and offered Office 365. Office 365 exists to take advantage of the cloud and comes with 1 TB of storage in the cloud. Not surprisingly, Microsoft offers several different subscription plans designed for business, each of which requires an annual commitment.

- The Business Essentials plan costs $5 per month per user. It affords an online version of Office with e-mail and video conferencing. It excludes use on tablets and phones.
- The 365 Business version costs $8.25 per user per month and allows use on tablets and smartphones but excludes use of the video conferencing, e-mail, calendar, and contact features.
- The 365 Business Premium version costs $12.50 per user per month and includes all the available features (including tablet and phone use, e-mail, calendar, contacts, and video conferencing).

If you do not use Outlook as your mail/contacts/calendar program, you should be fine with the Business version. If you do, you will want the Business Premium version. If you have Microsoft Office on your computer already, Microsoft has made it necessary for you to get Office 365 for at least $8.25 per month, if you want to use Office directly on your tablet or smartphone. Without Office 365, Office files are available on a read-only basis to your mobile devices, unless you acquire one of the many work-alike Apps that exist to let you work with Office files on tablets without actually having Office on the tablet.

Having Office 365 does have some advantages. For example, Microsoft lets you install it on up to five devices per subscription. Additionally, you won't have to buy upgrades and new versions of the software; they will automatically install for you.

For now, Microsoft continues to sell local installations of the Office Suite. They have made it less favorable to purchase them, limiting them to a single PC and excluding the ability to use the software with a tablet or phone. We predict that, ultimately, the only way you will be able to get Office is via subscription.

FileMaker Pro

The evolution of software programming for computers and mobile devices has made it possible for you to find a program that will meet virtually any data organization need you have. Limiting yourself to someone else's database, however, means that sometimes you have to make do with something that does not exactly work the way you want. In that situation, you may want to create a solution that works as you want it to, rather than do it in a way that does not work well for you. The answer: Get a good relational database program and build your own solution.

For some time FileMaker has offered a reasonably priced, simple-to-use relational database that we think is the best in its class. File-Maker gives you the ability to create custom solutions that you can use to manage information on your desktop, laptop, iPad, or iPhone. FileMaker 14 is the most current version.

FileMaker comes with a library of solutions that may well contain what you need. You can easily modify the solutions from the library to tweak them to exactly what you need. You can check out some of the available solutions at www.filemaker.com/solutions.

If you do not find what you need in the library, FileMaker makes it easy to create your own solution from scratch.

FileMaker comes in several versions. We like Pro the best ($329). The Advanced version ($549) contains all of the features of File-Maker Pro and adds a collection of advanced features designed for more experienced users to assist in creating more sophisticated and customized solutions. The advanced features include (among others) debugging tools, the ability to create stand-alone runtime solutions (solutions that do not require a copy of FileMaker to run), and the ability to create custom functions (www.filemaker.com).

Credenza

If you are a Microsoft Outlook user and want to turn your Outlook into practice-management software, check out the Microsoft Outlook add-on Credenza. The software is from Gavel and Gown, the company behind Amicus Attorney. Credenza is an innovative practice-management solution that runs as part of Microsoft Outlook. It is a handy solution for lawyers, accountants, consultants, or other professionals who want to organize their information around client files, matters, or projects. Microsoft Outlook alone cannot do this. You can use Categories and tasks to some extent, but when it comes to organizing around matters and clients, Outlook falls short.

With Credenza, you can organize e-mails, appointments, tasks, documents, notes, research, and phone calls. Installation and setup is quick and easy, and the interface is highly customizable. You can organize new projects as a matter, file, case, project, or any other name you can come up with. You can set a default type of project or matter and add your own categories if they are not already listed.

There are two versions of Credenza available, Basic and Pro. Credenza Basic is a free Microsoft add-on. Basic allows you to use the e-mail management, calendaring, task management, contacts, notes, files, time sheets, and document-management features. Credenza Pro, which runs $24.95 per month per user, has all the basic features, plus you can share these features with members of your team. With Pro, you can also take calls and messages for other users when in a team and have access to cloud-based document management. Pro also allows you to use the add-on's invoice and billing features.

Credenza supports Outlook 2003, Outlook 2007, Outlook 2010 (32-Bit), and Outlook 2013 (32-Bit) on Windows XP, Windows Vista, Windows 7, and Windows 8. Since Credenza is an Outlook add-on, it will run on Mac computers if you set up a Windows environment with Outlook installed using Parallels or some other windows system emulator or Bootcamp. Using Credenza will not corrupt your Outlook data storage; the add-on uses a separate SQL CE database to keep its data separate.

Send a Fax without a Fax Machine

The traditional office may have a dedicated fax machine, or a multifunction fax printer, but if you want to save money on installing a dedicated fax line, not to mention saving shelf space, you can turn your PC into a fax machine. Years ago, the fastest way to get a document into the hands of your opposing counsel or colleagues who were out of the office was to fax it. Today, it is much faster to scan a document as a PDF and send it, or send it in its original file format if it is still in the editing process.

Occasionally, though, some services (arguably archaic ones) only communicate via fax. Sometimes you will have clients who are more comfortable with a fax machine than with a scan and e-mail system. In any case, it pays to be flexible, and you can easily set up a fax-to-e-mail/e-mail-to-fax system. If you find yourself in a bind, needing to send a fax from somewhere without a fax machine you can access, you are still in good shape so long as you have Internet access. Here are a few Web-based fax services that can get your document out in a pinch:

- Sfax
- Secure Fax by Innoport
- RingCentral
- MetroFax

When choosing a service, some of the standard features you should expect include the following:

- customized cover pages
- delivery notifications of faxes
- fax logs

Let's take Sfax as an example. With this service, you can send an e-mail directly to a fax number, fax to multiple recipients, and receive e-mail notifications upon delivery of a fax. The online faxing service has auto resend should a fax fail to send and mobile fax alerts. There is an option for international faxing available on certain plans.

Most of these services are very intuitive and easy to set up. For example, with RingCentral, as with other services, you can send a fax via e-mail using the fax number (do not include "1") @rcfax.com, or you can send via Web, mobile, or desktop Apps.

Security and Ethics

Security and ethics have a significant interrelationship and we have combined the two for presentation in this book. We have done that because lawyers must consider the ethical consequences of using technology, as well as the ethical issues associated with failing to use technology. When making that analysis, the consequences of not using technology make the decision to use it fairly simple. Once a lawyer decides to make use of technology on a professional basis, the decision demands the use of competent security measures.

The implementation of appropriate security measures affects lawyers on a personal as well as a professional level. On a personal level, you will want to protect your own information from the bad guys to ensure that you do not become a victim of identity theft or have other problems associated with theft of your personal information. On a professional level, attorneys have an ethical obligation to protect clients' confidential information.

Certainly ethical obligations extend beyond the implementation of proper security measures, but when it comes to using technology and making information available through the Internet, there is no more important topic. Accordingly, most of our tips in this section relate to data protection.

Metadata: Know What You Are Sending in Microsoft Word

Microsoft Word's Track Changes feature is a handy tool, especially if you collaborate while drafting documents. It is the digital equivalent of red-lining a document. It allows you to see the changes that different users have made, and even notes which user made the change. However, it can pose a risk of accidentally disclosing confidential information. With Track Changes enabled, any changes (deletions, insertions, formatting, etc.) that you make in a document are recorded. If you delete a sentence, it shows up in a different color with a strike-through indicating the language was removed. You can enable Track Changes without viewing the track-change history to make it easier to read and edit, but you have to remember to go back and accept all the changes to the document before you send it, or the recipient can simply turn on the change view and see everything you deleted. So if you included confidential information in your earlier drafts and delete before sending, your recipient may still be able to view what was in the document earlier by switching on the Track Changes view. The ABA's Legal Technology Resource Center has compiled a listing of Ethics Opinions across the United States on the issue of metadata. Based on Model Rule of Professional Conduct 1.6, it is the sending lawyer's responsibility to scrub out the metadata before sending a document. Rule 1.6(C) provides: "A lawyer shall make reasonable efforts to prevent the inadvertent or unauthorized disclosure of, or unauthorized access to, information relating to the representation of a client."

Comment 18 to this rule elaborates:

[18] Paragraph (c) requires a lawyer to act competently to safeguard information relating to the representation of a client against unauthorized access by third parties and against inadvertent or unauthorized disclosure by the lawyer or other persons who are participating in the representation of the client or who are subject to the lawyer's supervision. See Rules 1.1, 5.1 and 5.3. The unauthorized access to, or the inadvertent or unauthorized disclosure of, information relating to the representation of a client does not constitute a violation of paragraph (c) if the lawyer has made reasonable efforts to prevent

the access or disclosure. Factors to be considered in determining the reasonableness of the lawyer's efforts include, but are not limited to, the sensitivity of the information, the likelihood of disclosure if additional safeguards are not employed, the cost of employing additional safeguards, the difficulty of implementing the safeguards, and the extent to which the safeguards adversely affect the lawyer's ability to represent clients (e.g., by making a device or important piece of software excessively difficult to use). A client may require the lawyer to implement special security measures not required by this Rule or may give informed consent to forgo security measures that would otherwise be required by this Rule. Whether a lawyer may be required to take additional steps to safeguard a client's information in order to comply with other law, such as state and federal laws that govern data privacy or that impose notification requirements upon the loss of, or unauthorized access to, electronic information, is beyond the scope of these Rules.

You can activate a setting in Microsoft Word to help with this responsibility. Word has a feature that will warn you before you print, save, or send a file that contains tracked changes.
In Word 2010–2013:

Step one: Go to File → Options → Trust Center
Step two: Go into Trust Center Settings → Privacy Options
Step three: Check the box that says, "Warn before printing, saving, or sending a file that contains tracked changes or comments"

Once you have enabled this option, a warning message will appear if you click to save or save as, print to a physical printer or to PDF, save to PDF or use a PDF conversion tool like Acrobat or Nuance, or use any command under the "Save and Send" menu. Be mindful that this is not a foolproof system; if you attach the file from within your e-mail program, you will get no notice.

Password Protect

Your Devices, Information, and Files

To protect your privacy and your clients' confidential communications, you should make it a point to password-protect your files and your devices to preclude easy access by the prying eyes of the bad guys.

1. Virtually all smartphones, tablets, and contemporary computers allow the creation of some form of access code ranging from biometric scanning to a defined finger swipe to a code number to more complex passwords.
2. You should enable such security measures and implement them on all of your devices.
3. You can secure documents when not in use by compressing and encrypting them and assigning a password to the encrypted file that prevents access to the file without the password. It is also possible to employ the process to a large number of documents compiled into a single file or encompassed by a single folder.
4. You can protect your information by adopting secure passwords for all of your online accounts containing private information.

Remember that the weakest link in any chain will always be the weakest link in the chain and the most likely point of attack by the bad guys.

Use Strong Passwords

By now most of us know to use passwords to protect our bank, e-mail, and other accounts, and access to our computers and mobile devices. Many of us also know about using them to protect encrypted files. The use of passwords to access everything tends to make us want to use a simple password that we can easily remember and to use it for most, if not all, of our accounts.

Unfortunately, using a simple password makes it easier for the bad guys to determine the password and access information, files, and devices. Stay away from simple or weak passwords. Opt for stronger ones and do not use the same password for all of your accounts. If you have password requirements for accounts that do not acquire information you must or simply want to keep confidential, you can use the same password for several such accounts. If you do that, however, don't use the same password for anything that can access confidential or private information. While it may prove more difficult to keep track of a collection of passwords, software can help you do that. See other tips respecting some recommendations. Here are some guidelines and examples for passwords:

- Weak passwords:
  - An example of a weak password: password
  - Don't use your name, initials, birthdate, address, etc.
  - Don't use anything easily associated with you.
- Strong passwords:
  - An example of a strong password: 297Puj548iXU@!
  - Random characters work well, but use at least eight of them.
  - Mix alphanumeric-symbolic characters and capitals/lowercase.
- Passphrases work best (longer is better):
  - An example of a passphrase: 496BewareTheJabberwok!!!
  - Even with a longer passphrase, mix alphanumeric-symbolic characters and capitals/lowercase letters.

Keep Your Passwords Secure

No matter how good a job you do choosing a strong password, the effort amounts to nothing if you do not appropriately secure your password. Over the years we have seen all manners of storing passwords—some better than others. Some password storage we have seen is so bad it is most charitably described as "negligent." Among the really bad ideas we have seen:

- Writing the password on a sticky note and putting it on the computer monitor.
- Writing the password on a 3″ x 5″ card or a piece of paper and jamming it into the side of a desk blotter.
- Setting a screen saver to flash the password on the screen.

- Pinning the password to a corkboard on the wall of a secretary's cubicle.
- Deciding that passwords create too much hassle and removing the protection from the computer, tablet, or smartphone.

Use Biometric Security

More and more companies have come to the conclusion that biometric devices provide the best means of security/access. Although technically not a password, they function similarly in terms of access to the file.

Biometric devices usually use fingerprint scanners, although some of the more sophisticated versions use retinal scans. Biometric devices sometimes come attached to a device, such as part of the DNA of the iPhone and the newer iPads or as a fingerprint scanner built into a laptop computer or a keyboard. Other devices come separately and connect upon attachment to the computer, often via a USB port.

We have found that the newer biometric devices (usually a fingerprint scanner) work fairly reliably. Most offer a backup option of password entry if the biometrics don't allow access. We have found that the biometric devices have grown more reliable in recent years and we are now advocates of using them, when they are available. Even if you have a biometric device, the system will likely have you set a backup password; be sure to keep the guidelines we suggested for strong passwords in mind.

1Password

As our lives become more complex and our Internet dependence more complete, we tend to accumulate more than an insignificant number of passwords to allow us to access our files, devices, and information.

We want to use strong passwords to protect confidential information and don't want to duplicate use of the same passwords for different accounts; remembering all of the passwords becomes an almost insurmountable task for most people. To assist us in this feat, a number of vendors have devised database programs to keep track of the information. Some of them will even auto-fill it for you on cue. The concept of these programs is that you remember the password to access the file and it remembers all of your other passwords for you. All in all, we find that to be a neat and very useful trick.

Many of these programs allow installation on numerous devices and move the information about your passwords from one entry point to all the devices connected to your account, making it incredibly useful and easier to use. We have found several programs of this ilk that we like, including one of our favorites, 1Password by Agilebits (www.agilebits.com).

Password Meter

This program lets you test your chosen passwords to determine how secure they are. The program does not guarantee accuracy in its evaluation, but because of the markers it uses, you likely enhance your security by using a password rated highly by the program. You can access it at www.passwordmeter.com.

How Secure Is My Password?

How Secure Is My Password? is another online password-checking program. It cleverly provides you with an estimate as to how long contemporary password-cracking software would require to breach your security and crack your password. The program generated an estimate that it would take four thousand years for the current generation of password-cracker software to come up with a password used by one of the authors. While the time required certainly gives us a sense of confidence in the security of the password choice, we honestly believe that anything over 1,000 years is just bragging.

Stop Using TrueCrypt

You can find many programs to encrypt your data. Some software comes with its own encryption and passcode structure. Some operating systems include the ability to condense file folders filled with data, encrypt them, and password-protect them. You can also get third-party software to provide those capabilities.

TrueCrypt was a good source of quality encryption software for a long time. Many attorneys used it, largely because it was both reliable and free. In fact, for some time we recommended using it in many of our tech tips. The world has changed and now we have to advise you not to use it. The developer of TrueCrypt stopped supporting the program when Microsoft announced that it would no longer support Windows XP in 2014. As a result, no effort has been made to protect the software against more recent threats and we now consider it unreliable and untrustworthy.

Rather than run with out-of-date software, if you used TrueCrypt, you should retrieve your data from it and re-encrypt it with another software that is currently supported. You can find help in the first part of the conversion at the former TrueCrypt site, which forwards you to http://truecrypt.sourceforge.net to receive instructions for Windows users for de-encrypting a drive and migrating to another encryption system. Although the instructions are for BitLocker, you do not have to go to that system.

PAY HEED TO THE FOLLOWING WARNING THAT APPEARS ON THE SITE:

> "WARNING: Using TrueCrypt is not secure as it may contain unfixed security issues"

If you use any platform other than Windows, go to http://true crypt.sourceforge.net/OtherPlatforms.html.

limit Your Exposure: Avoid Public Wi-Fi

Public Wi-Fi connections expose you to greater risk than secure private connections. The reason for that is that the public Wi-Fi connections present a shared network that allows strangers to potentially gain access to your electronics joined on the shared network. Public hotspots include the free connections at coffee shops and the connections (free or paid for) at hotels, on airplanes, etc. You can limit your exposure and maintain contact in most cases by carrying your own secure cellular-based hotspot (see the Hardware section for information about the Mi-Fi and other similar devices).

We do not deny the superficial convenience of logging onto a public connection and not having to worry about whether you remembered to charge your cellular hotspot, or that free is initially less costly than buying a cellular hotspot and subscribing to a data connection for it with a provider. On the other hand, the cost in time, hassle, inconvenience, and, ultimately, money resulting from a data security breach allowed by your use of a public Wi-Fi network far outweighs the initial savings.

To make the point, we logged into the public Wi-Fi network in our hotel during a recent trip. It was early in the morning, so there was not much activity on the network, but we found enough to make the point. The following screen capture shows the other computers attached to the network and highlights one traveling so unprotected that, had we wanted to, we could have simply and easily connected to the computer and accessed its content.

Protect yourself. Protect your clients. Protect your data. Keep away from public Wi-Fi. If you find yourself in a situation where you have to use public Wi-Fi (e.g., you are out of the country and your cellular connection does not work there), limit your exposure by doing the following things:

1. Take clients' confidential information as an encrypted file on a thumb drive and keep it separate from and off of your computer, except when you have to access it.

2. Do not access it while you are online, connected to the public network. Before you reconnect, re-encrypt the file on your thumb drive and disconnect it from your computer, then erase it from your computer.

3. Do not do anything financial on the public network. That means do not access your bank accounts; do not pay your bills; do not access your brokerage accounts (you get the picture).

4. If you have to use a public network, you can limit your exposure significantly by using a VPN (Virtual Private Network) to provide some cloaking to your presence. Note that you will need to get the VPN set up before you connect to the public Wi-Fi if you want to use it in connection with the VPN.

You Need Privacy When You Work

We all know that lawyers have an ethical obligation to protect their clients' confidential information and their communications with their clients. They teach us that practically the first day of law school, but most of us learned from TV before we ever started law school. While many of our clients may lack experience and sophistication, almost all of them know that communications with their attorney have the cloak of confidentiality. That said, now that we live in the information age, lawyers can and do work almost anywhere. We have seen lawyers working on airplanes, in airports, on trains, in train stations, on various local public transportation systems, in restaurants, in bars, at sporting events, in shopping centers, and at a variety of conventions, seminars, and other public settings of almost any and all varieties. We should not have to point out the risks associated with such conduct in terms of a third party seeing what you have on the screen of your mobile device or overhearing your conversation. Nevertheless, the frequency of these occurrences requires that we address the issue.

The failure to protect your clients' confidential communications can result in disciplinary proceedings regarding your license to practice law. It can, in some cases, also create civil liability. Accordingly, as tempting as we may find it to get a bit of work done while sipping coffee at our favorite coffee shop or while we travel, we need to restrain that impulse. If you cannot or do not wish to avoid working in those situations, you need to take steps to protect yourself and your client. While we favor taking a break from work to help preserve mental health and psychological well-being, we recognize that lawyers will be lawyers and work will get done in those situations from time to time. We will even admit that we occasionally do it.

If you intend to work in public environments, you need to take steps to reduce the likelihood of someone seeing or hearing your activities. You can limit your exposure by adopting the following guidelines:

1. Try to find a place to work where others cannot easily ascertain what you are doing. For example, in a restaurant, sit with your back to a wall, so someone will not stand behind you and have the ability to read your laptop screen, tablet screen, phone display, or notepad.

2. Avoid working on matters involving confidential communications while in public places.

3. Use privacy screens on your electronic devices (several companies make filters that you can place over your display so that the display can only be read by someone looking directly at it straight on and not from off to the side, such as the next seat in an airplane).

4. Avoid talking on the phone in public places. Use an earphone when others are around. If you are in a public place, try to limit your calls to nonconfidential matters and schedule a private time to discuss private things.

Enable Auto-Lock and Add a Passcode

Auto-Lock is your first line of defense in mobile data privacy. It is also the easiest line of defense to set up.

For iOS users, enabling your Auto-Lock features along with a passcode is enough to apply the significant security measures that Apple implemented in their iOS platform. If you already have iOS 8 or its later iterations on your phone, Auto-Lock was automatically enabled when you first set the phone up. If you are on an earlier-generation iOS, then you can enable the Auto-Lock feature through your Settings menu by tapping the General button. You can also choose how much time may lapse before the phone is auto-locked, with choices from one to five minutes or never. Setting it for one minute means you will activate security features faster and save on battery life.

If you tap your way back to the Settings menu, you will notice the fourth button down from the General menu is the Passcode menu; tap the Passcode button to open up a list of options. Here you can turn on your passcode, change it, dictate how long before the passcode is activated, and decide whether to use a simple passcode consisting of four numerical digits or turn this feature off to use as complicated a passcode as you can tolerate. The combination of letters, numbers, and special characters you can employ is virtually endless. The authors tested a 50-character passcode, and the iPhone took it (though we don't believe yours needs to be quite this long). With a four-digit numeric passcode and 10 numerical options, there are potentially 10,000 different passcode options. Switch to a six-character complex passcode, and you have 77 options when you consider all the numbers, letters, and special characters. This increases your options from 10,000 to 208.4 billion, significantly increasing the security your passcode offers.

For Android users, the process will depend upon which version of the Android system you have. By way of example, in the very popular Jelly Bean version (Android v. 4.1), you will go from the Home Screen to Apps by tapping the icon. Then go to "Settings" and then to "Security & Screen Lock." You will have the following options:

- Slide: No protection, but you get to the Home screen quickly.
- Face Unlock: You unlock your phone by looking at it. This is the least secure lock.

- Pattern: You draw a simple pattern, like the number "6" with your finger to unlock the phone. This is slightly more secure than Face Unlock.
- PIN: You choose four or more numbers. Longer PINs tend to be more secure.
- Password: Requires four or more characters. This is the most secure option, as long as you create a strong password.

Turn Off Bluetooth When Not in Use

Bluetooth is a great convenience. It allows us to wirelessly connect our smartphones, tablets, and other devices to each other, our cars, speaker-phones, speakers, and headsets. Although it met some resistance when it first came out, it has now received general and widespread acceptance. Virtually every smartphone (and a lot of not-so-smart phones), tablets, and many other mobile devices come with Bluetooth technology. We like Bluetooth and encourage you to use it for convenient connections to many accessory devices. But, as with most technology, it has a downside. If your device is always Bluetooth-discoverable, you expose yourself to malicious actors who can access your device and communications. Once they have access, they can send viruses and use your phone to make calls, among other unwanted activities.

A recent evolution of Bluetooth convenience has made the situation more precarious. When it first came out, most Bluetooth connections required you to enter a code to make the connection. That had the benefit of giving you a chance to reject the connection, even if most of the codes were "000" or "0000." Now many devices will pair automatically to your device without the entry of a code. While you can still check to see what devices are paired and remove those you do not want, automatic pairing does increase the risk of inappropriate access. The trade-off of security for convenience comes with many dangers. The best defense to this is to turn Bluetooth discoverability off when you are not trying to pair a device. An additional benefit of turning pairing off is that keeping it on when you don't need it will drain your battery life.

Protect against Cell Phone Viruses

There are a host of antivirus software options available for Android phone users. Google, unlike Apple, doesn't vet applications before they go live on Google Play. This has proved to be an easy way for malware creators to use the Google App store to launch their malicious Apps. Along with antivirus and malware scanning, security Apps for Android also offer a full security suite with features such as device location, remote wipe, backup, and suspicious-URL blocking. These extra features usually require a premium subscription, but most Apps offer a basic level of protection for free, including malware scanning. The backup features in security Apps can save your data if that data is not automatically backed up to Google.

Lookout Security & Antivirus is an Android App that offers a good selection of security features and works well; but some users have reported that it results in a more rapid battery drain than normally should occur. We had the program installed for several months on a Samsung Galaxy S5 and did not notice a significant difference in battery life.

Keep Your Software Up to Date

Many people think that if their computer or mobile device works, they don't need to update the operating system or program software. WRONG! The bad guys constantly look for weaknesses in software that will enable them to access computers to wreak their havoc. Software developers issue updates for a variety of reasons. Sometimes the updates cure problems in the operation of the software, sometimes they add new features, and sometimes they close security holes that enable the bad guys to get into computers and/or mobile devices.

Regularly checking for and installing updates can provide new features for you and also enhance the security of your system and device.

We sympathize with those of you who hesitate to mess with something that works. We have been burned on more than one occasion by a prematurely released update that is less than ready for prime time. The good news is that we have had no problems with the overwhelming majority of the updates that we have installed from responsible and well-established vendors. We won't endeavor to list all the vendors from whom we have installed software updates with and without problems, as we have not maintained those records. We will tell you that we have had issues with installations from all major vendors, including Microsoft and Apple. That said, we continue to recommend that you keep your software (and in particular your operating systems) current, especially with respect to security issues. We do offer one suggestion in the interests of self-preservation: when a new fix comes out, you do not have to install it before anyone else does.

Wait a few days and check to see if people have reported any problems with it. Then you can decide to move forward or wait. There have been times when that approach saved considerable trouble as a vendor released an update, discovered an issue, and then released a fix for it shortly thereafter. We have seen that happen more than once and have also seen releases followed by several corrective patches and updates within a very short period of time following the initial release. By waiting until the update or upgrade stabilized, we avoided the problems of the initial release.

Similarly, when a company stops supporting a particular version of its operating system or software, stop using it. We recently had that experience with Windows XP when Microsoft announced that it would no longer support it, which meant that it would not offer any new corrections for vulnerability problems. If any of you continue to use Windows XP, we recommend that you immediately upgrade to a newer version of Windows.

Back Up Essential Files

Make it a practice to keep multiple current backup copies of your data to ensure against loss. Common sense and safety dictate that you should have at least one of the backup copies in a safe and secure location outside of your office. We like redundancy when it comes to backups as it gives us security against failure of one of the backups. But you must understand that it does not make any difference how many backup copies you have if you store them all in the same place and they all get destroyed in a common disaster, such as a fire. You should have at least three backup copies of all critical data and you should store at least one copy in a secure location apart from the other copies. We like the idea of having four copies, two in the office, one that lives in a briefcase, and a fourth in a secure location outside of the office. A fifth in a separate secure location outside of the office would not hurt anything. The good news is that the cost of the backup drives has grown increasingly less expensive and the process of backing up has become both easy and reliable. In the old days we used to back up to tape systems that proved hard to work with and slow and often failed. Now we back up much more easily to hard disks, many of which are sufficiently small as to make them easily transportable. Another approach becoming more and more common is to back up to the cloud (a remote storage system to which you connect). We like using the cloud as an emergency backup. We us it as a redundant backup as it is slower and less convenient than a physical drive, but it stores our data in a remote location so that it is unlikely that a common disaster would befall it and our local physical backups.

When it comes to backing up, you should include all important data, such as client files, accounting records, documents, etc. We like using physical backups as they allow more rapid restoration than the cloud. We like using the cloud as it gives us geographic security and redundancy. Bottom line: use both. Let the cloud be a "last resort" if you lose physical backups for any reason.

As a practical matter, you help yourself stay in business by also backing up your applications. If you have a catastrophic failure of your computer (or more likely its storage drive), that will enable you to get back up and running much more quickly than reinstalling all of your programs. We use a desktop computer at the office and keep duplicates of the software and the data on a laptop that leaves the office with us each day. That enables us to do our work almost anywhere and rapidly and easily restore information from one place to another should data be lost due to a disaster. We also use a backup system that clones the computer hard drive and allows replacement of the entire drive or any piece of data separately. For those of you using Apple, the Time Machine backup feature built into OS X works very well and has proven reliable.

Encrypt Important and Confidential Data

Make it a point to encrypt confidential data to ensure protection from hackers and other bad guys. Failing to encrypt confidential data could create an ethical problem for you as an attorney. Failing to encrypt nonconfidential data might cause other problems for you if it is important, as its ready accessibility makes it more susceptible to theft and corruption. Accordingly, encryption of all important and confidential data is a good ("best") practice. If you regularly encrypt all your files, you ensure that you don't miss one that you should encrypt.

When you encrypt, use 256-bit encryption and a strong password or passphrase. Remember that when it comes to passwords: (1) longer is stronger, (2) a combination of lower- and uppercase letters offer more security than one or the other, (3) alphanumeric passwords provide better security than either strictly alphabetical or exclusively numeric passwords, (4) adding one or more symbols to the alpha and numeric characters strengthens your password even more.

If encryption puts your information in a virtual safe (or at least a safe condition), think of the password as the lock and key. You will have much better protection from a well-built lock than by twisting a paper clip or a piece of wire to hold the latch in place.

Redundancy Is Not Always Bad

While we can probably agree that we should try to avoid redundancy in our writing, we should absolutely all agree that having redundant backups to your computer data can save your professional life. We recommend that you have at least three different backups of your data, that you keep them current, and that you keep them in different places. Within reason, more is better. By way of example, we keep multiple copies of our data and our software: Data files are duplicated twice in physical files that live in the office, once more on a drive that leaves the office with us, and twice more in the cloud (more about that later). Clones of the entire computer drive exist in the office and in a drive that leaves the office, but not in the cloud, both due to the fact that storing that much information in the cloud would take far too long to get up and downloaded to make it reasonable and due to the fact that program files are generally fairly easily replaced. By the way, try to make your redundancy include both physical backups and the cloud. Include geographical redundancy in your planning to protect against losing all of your backups in the same disaster.

DocuSign

As lawyers strive to circulate less and less paper in their offices, services like DocuSign become increasingly handier. At $10 per month (paid annually), users can send up to five documents for electronic signature per month. Need more than that? For $20 per month (paid annually), you may have up to ten users send an unlimited number of documents for electronic signature. DocuSign will store your completed signed documents for retrieval from anywhere you find yourself working. You can automate your repetitive documents, such as client retainer letters, to deliver documents to your clients and get their signatures faster. You can save money and time by avoiding the costs of overnighting documents back and forth or printing and faxing. Client satisfaction improves as your clients no longer have to arrange their schedules to come into the office and sign documents. If you are curious about the legality of electronic signatures, Docu-Sign answers your questions at https://www.docusign.com/electronic -signature-legality. According to their site:

> There are two Acts that establish the legality of electronic signatures in the United States—the Electronic Signatures in Global and National Commerce Act (ESIGN, 2000) and the Uniform Electronic Transactions Act (UETA, 1999). Both ESIGN and UETA establish that electronic records and signatures carry the same weight and legal effect as traditional paper documents and handwritten signatures stating: A document or signature cannot be denied legal effect or enforceability solely because it is in electronic form.

With the legality and enforceability in place, using services like DocuSign to speed up your delivery and cut down your paper clutter just makes sense.

Security on the Go

- Password-protect your mobile phone/tablet/laptops.
- Do not use an unsecured public Wi-Fi to access your e-mail or data.
- Disable Bluetooth on your phone until you need it or make your device undiscoverable.
- Do not leave your mobile device unattended (even for a minute).
- Do not ask a stranger to watch your mobile device while you go to the bathroom, get a refill on your coffee, or attend to any other matter.

Prevent Identity Theft: Use Apple Pay

If you have a newer iPhone (5s or later), you can connect many of your credit cards to the Apple Pay system. To the extent that you can use Apple Pay, you reduce your exposure to identity theft and theft of your credit card. The system provides greater security than the physical card; and you can have several of them connected to your Apple Pay account. (Note: you can use Apple Pay with any iOS device that has a finger print reader, including the iPad Air 2 and iPad Mini 3). Apple Pay will also work with the Apple Watch. You get Apple Pay through the Apple Wallet App. In addition to credit cards, you can also add airline boarding passes and event tickets to your account.

Apple Pay's security results from several factors. First, Apple Pay does not work until you verify that you are you with your finger or thumbprint. Once you have done that, Apple Pay processes the transaction. In processing, Apple Pay does not transmit your full account number in connection with transactions. Rather, it creates a new number keyed exclusively to your device and transmits that number. Apple does not store your account information on its computers.

While we like Apple Pay very much, we do want to make sure that you understand its limitations. First of all, not all banks coordinate with Apple Pay. If your bank does not work with Apple Pay, you won't be able to get your credit card issued by that bank on the Apple Pay account. Second, some banks allow only some credit cards to work with Apple Pay. For example, at this time Chase allows personal credit cards to connect to Apple Pay, but it does not allow business accounts to connect. Third, you can get away with not carrying most of your cards, but you should carry at least one physical card, as not all vendors accept Apple Pay. It requires a reader that not all vendors have acquired as yet.

Crack Down on Spam in Your Inbox

According to Kaspersky, a leader in protection solutions, in 2013 the percent of mail traffic that consisted of spam rose 4 percent to a staggering 70 percent. Spam is a pain to weed through and a huge drain on time. Anything that interferes with handling e-mail is a burden and an additional cost of doing business. Here are some ways to deal with the unnecessary junk.

1. Outlook users should update their junk e-mail filter. (You can get the latest update to your junk e-mail filters at https://support.microsoft.com/en-us/kb/872976.)
2. Check out Cloudmark DesktopOne. DesktopOne works with your favorite e-mail programs, such as Microsoft Outlook, Outlook Express, Mozilla Thunderbird, and more. The free version will automatically filter through one e-mail account.
3. If you use a Web designer, consider having them embed your e-mail in a way that impedes spammers from harvesting it.
4. Responding to links on spam e-mail messages to "Click on this link to unsubscribe to these great offers" doesn't always do the trick. Although some are legitimate, most just verify your e-mail address as being "live," making it more certain that you will receive more spam from this and other spammers.

Following some best practices may help cut down on the amount of spam you endure. First, keep a personal e-mail address for friends and family, and make a point to never list it on a website, use it to order something on the Internet, or otherwise make it public. Second, you should keep a business e-mail address that you put on your business card, give to your clients and others that you expect to correspond with, but again, never list on a website, use to order something on the Internet, or otherwise make public. You may want to consider a disposable e-mail address (DEA) service. A DEA is a special e-mail address that you obtain from a DEA provider. E-mail addressed to you via the DEA is sent to the DEA provider and then forwarded to your real e-mail address. The sender has no idea what your real e-mail address is. If you respond to the e-mail, it is routed through the DEA provider, so when the original sender receives your reply, the sending address is the DEA. There are several such service providers out there, including:

- Spamex
- Mailinator
- Guerilla Mail

Travel Tips

There was a time when people enjoyed the experience of traveling. We used to even see ads from the travel industry telling us that getting to our destination was half the fun. For most of us, however, in recent years, travel has become a pain in the posterior portion of our anatomy. While we travel both for business and pleasure, unfortunately, we have attended some meetings that were bad enough that getting there was still half the fun.

Lawyers may spend most of their time in their office, but they also travel both for professional and personal reasons. Travel has become more complicated than it used to be and now often presents more of a challenge. In this section, we will provide some tips that you may find helpful with respect to your travels. The tips in this section should help you save time and/or money or just make things a little easier for you when you travel. We have found that they work well for us and hope that they work well for you as well. Please also see the section on security and ethics, as many tips located in that section bear on the use of technology in the course of your travels.

FareCompare

Farecompare.com is an airfare comparison site. It provides real-time price quotes across 500-plus airlines. This is a handy tool when you are in the early stages of planning your trip. You can search for one-way or round-trip fares. All you have to do is enter your originating city and destination city, along with the dates of travel. You then select which airfare sites you would like to compare. Farecompare .com will do an aggregate search across a multitude of sites to pull the data on flights, saving you the time of going site to site. Once you have identified the best rate, you should close out your Internet, clear the cookies in your Internet browser, then go back to that site, or the airline directly, to book your flight. Some websites will track how many times you access the site, and the flight cost will go up as a result. Clearing the cookies prevents this tracking.

If you want to save on airfare and have some flexibility on your travel dates, it typically costs less to fly on Tuesdays, Wednesdays, and Saturdays.

Bonus Tip: Want the Internet to do the searching for you? Once you have an idea of when and where you want to fly to, sign up for a price-drop alert on Airfare Watchdog. Just go to www.airfare-watchdog.com and enter your travel details (originating airport, destination airport, travel dates, etc.) and how often you want to be notified about fares, and Airfare Watchdog will send you e-mail notices whenever there is a sale for your route.

FlightBoard

You can find any number of travel Apps for your smartphone or tablet at the Apple iTunes App Store, the Google Play Store, and other locations. Many of them actually can prove helpful to you on your journeys. FlightBoard gives you the equivalent of personal airport arrival and departure displays on your phone or tablet. You select the airport you want to use, and it gives you current information about arrivals and departures from that airport. You can narrow the focus from the date by time and airline until you find your flight, and then you can expand the information about your flight.

You choose among over 3,000 airports by touching the word "Airports" in the top left of the display (see image) and then typing the city or airport identification code ("San Francisco" and "SFO" both get you there). You can easily and instantly switch from arrivals to departures with the touch of a finger (see the arrows in the upper-right corner of the image). Note that there is another similar App called Flight Board. It is also a good App, but we prefer this one. This one also won the 2012 Webby Award for Best Travel App.

Flight Update Pro

Flight Update comes in a standard and a Pro version. The standard version costs $4.99 at the iTunes App Store. You can get the Pro version directly from the App Store or as an in-App upgrade for $5.99. The Pro version gets you push notifications of flight alerts and gate changes, includes non-direct flights when searching by route, and allows you to download flights directly from TripIt, if you link the two accounts. The App provides information about the airport, the weather, the location of your seat on the plane, and information about the equipment that will be used on your flight as it moves toward your departure point. It also gives you detailed information respecting the flight and keeps you up to date on the departure gate. We have found the App well designed, very useful, and highly functional. As we use TripIt regularly, we particularly like the fact that you can avoid manually entering the details about your flight by linking the account to TripIt and letting TripIt transfer the data to it. Note that the transfer is one way. You must provide the information to TripIt first if you want the information to transfer to the second App. If you send it to Flight Updater Pro first, it will not transfer automatically to TripIt.

TripIt

Get TripIt! TripIt works like a personal assistant to organize your travel information. You can access it almost anywhere as it connects to computers through your browser (www.tripit.com) or through most mobile devices. You can e-mail your flight, hotel, and confirmations to TripIt, and it will appear in your travel calendar (which you can publish to your primary calendar and share with others). You can build itineraries including maps and directions as well. You have your choice of three versions: a free version, TripIt Pro, and TripIt for Teams. We have not looked at TripIt for Teams, as it is too expensive, in our opinion ($29/mo.), and does not have as many features as TripIt Pro.

The free version gives you all the basics, but we particularly like the Pro version ($48/year). The Pro version adds several features to the basic package, including automatic sharing, alternate flight location, mobile alerts about flight changes, and flight refunds. The refund feature is worth the price of admission all by itself. Just to give you an idea, I purchased tickets for my wife and myself on a major carrier. Then I signed up for TripIt Pro and sent the flight information in to my account for inclusion on my travel calendar and with respect to that particular trip. About three months later, I got a notice from TripIt that the airline had reduced the fare by $200/person. TripIt recommended that I return the tickets and get new ones at the reduced price. Not a bad strategy, but for the fact that the airline would have charged a fee that would have wiped out much of the savings. Having learned of the reduced fare, however, I called the airline and we agreed that they would issue a $200 travel credit to each of us for use in a future ticket purchase. While I did not exactly follow TripIt's advice, without TripIt Pro, I may not have learned of the reduction. The $400 savings realized on that one trip paid for almost nine years of TripIt Pro.

You can access TripIt on your computer, iOS, Android, Blackberry, and Windows Phone devices. You can also add a TripIt calendar to your calendaring system, allowing you to have all your travel information in one place without the rest of your schedule (that makes it particularly painless if you want to share with family or friends).

Buy Smart

We did some research into the timeworn question about what days are the cheapest to fly on and when you are best advised to book a flight. This is what we found out. Best days to fly (least expensive) generally are Tuesday, Wednesday, and Saturday. Worst (most expensive) are Friday and Sunday. The best buys in airfares generally occur between one and three months prior to departure for domestic fights and five to six months before departure for international flights. Avoid buying a ticket within a week of departure if at all possible, as that is when business travelers get hit with premium prices for last-minute travel. The best time to buy a ticket is on Tuesdays after 3:00 p.m. We are advised that airlines often make fare reductions at this time. We know you do not always have the flexibility to buy in these time frames, but when you do, you can get substantial savings.

Do take note of the fact that the information in the preceding paragraph does not mean that you will get inexpensive fares. Airfares have generally been increasing recently, and airlines have imposed many hidden costs by separating out and charging for things that previously cost nothing, in order to make you believe that you are paying less than you really are to fly. Good examples include food service, checked baggage charges, and charges to go from ultra-cramped to merely cramped leg space on some flights.

In planning your travel, you should also take into consideration the fact that travel to certain places simply costs more in certain time frames and, with respect to certain holidays, can become extremely expensive. Airfare to a resort destination during the peak of tourist season at that location will always cost more than in shoulder seasons (just before or after the peak season) or in the off-season. Travel around Christmas generally costs more. Domestic travel around Thanksgiving also sees boosted fares. If you want to go to Rio for Carnival, expect to pay much more than you would have to pay at almost any other time of the year; same thing if you want to travel to the destination for the next World Cup Finals, Olympics, or Super Bowl around the time of those events.

Go Better with GOES

The Global Entry Travel System (GOES) allows you to clear customs coming back into the United States from international travel much more quickly, as you are a "known traveler" and they have vetted you sufficiently that they will give you the benefit of the doubt and presume that you are honest and safe, unless you give them reason to question that. If you have a GOES card, you get to use an automated kiosk to complete your customs declaration and go through an expedited reentry process. Check the GOES site (see next paragraph) for current information as to what airports offer this feature.

The process of getting a GOES card is relatively simple. You go online (https://goes-app.cbp.dhs.gov/main/goes), pay a $100 nonrefundable application fee, fill out an application, and wait for them to tell you whether you got preliminary approval or not. If you did get preliminary approval, you will need to schedule a personal interview so that they can see you are who you said you are. Don't wait until the last minute to do this, as while the preliminary approval process results came in relatively quickly, appointments for personal interviews take much longer. You can get the interview only at certain locations, and the waiting period generally runs two or three months. If you persevere, however, you may be able to get in sooner, as often appointments made several months ahead of time end up creating scheduling problems and get canceled for that or another reason. If you check back every once in a while, you may find that you can get an appointment slot that opened as a result of a cancelation on relatively short notice. Sometimes you can get an appointment in a matter of a week or two or possibly even a few days. You will need to bring your passport with you and some evidence of residence (like a utility bill).

A fringe benefit is that after you are approved, if you provide your GOES identification number when you purchase your tickets, you will get "TSA Pre" approval on your boarding passes on flights originating in the United States. Note, however, that not all U.S. airports have TSA Pre set up, and others may not offer it at all times.

For those unfamiliar with TSA Pre, it saves a fair amount of time and inconvenience during the check-in process. Most airports provide separate lines for TSA Pre customers. In that line, you do not have to get undressed, take your computer out of your briefcase, remove your toiletries from your suitcase, and then repack everything on the other side of the x-ray machine. You get to leave everything in place, go through, pick it up, and leave. There are some exceptions, however. If you have metal in your pockets, it has to come out; if you have too much metal in your belt buckle or watch, or metal in your shoes, you may have to remove them; and if you are wearing a heavy coat, you will have to send it through the machine separately (you do not have to remove light jackets, vests, or sweaters). It takes us about 25 percent of the time to get through the security clearance process with TSA Pre by comparison to the regular procedures (measured from arrival at the table next to the conveyor belt for the luggage x-ray machine).

Gate Guru

We all spend more time than we would like sitting in airport waiting rooms. Often we wonder what facilities will be near our gate. Would it work better to buy something to eat or a cup of coffee before we get to the gate or wait until we do? If we do not know the airport well, we take potluck, guessing at what we will find when we get to the gate. With Gate Guru, we get inside information. Gate Guru (available for iOS devices at the iTunes App Store) tells you where in the airport you will find what facilities. It will tell you where to get magazines, coffee, hamburgers, or hard liquor in the airport. In larger airports, it will give you the option of selecting by gate, by terminal, and by vendor. In addition, the App will provide you with maps of the airport, and now it also offers information as to departing and arriving flights. All of this functionality ought to cost something, but it is a free download from the App Store. Although we trust our own judgment more than CNN's when it comes to evaluating Apps, we never object to sharing CNN's opinion when it agrees with our own. CNN rated this a Top 5 Air Travel App.

Miscellaneous Tips

In trying to put together this collection of tips, we found a few that did not fit well into the categories we used to organize the tips. We still wanted to make these tips available to you, despite the fact that they did not fit into those categories. Accordingly, we created a section for miscellaneous tips. This section will include tips that we considered valuable but that did not fit into the other divisions.

The Art of Mobile Lawyering

To varying degrees, we have all adopted mobility as part of our practice. Almost no one practices law exclusively in his or her office. Most of us have meetings in clients' offices or other attorneys' offices; take work home; attend depositions, trials, or hearings outside of our office; or endeavor to do some work while we travel for work or pleasure.

In the bad old days, a lawyer out of the office worked under a serious handicap. The lawyer had few tools and less support outside of the office. We had no mobile phones, no Internet, no computers, etc. Now we have all of those things and more, and those tools make it far easier for a lawyer to work effectively and efficiently outside of the office.

As more and more mobile tools became available, many of us started collecting them and, to ensure that we had the ability to do all that the tools would allow, carried far more than we should have. Fortunately, someone came up with the idea of wheeled computer bags—or many more of us would have serious back problems today. Better mobility requires more discerning packing these days.

Remember Allen's First Law of Mobility. That law states: "Tools make you mobile by helping you work efficiently and effectively on the road, but the more you carry with you, the less mobile you become."

Every physical tool, no matter how small, takes up space. Every physical tool, no matter how light, adds weight. Schlepping a lot of equipment around makes it hard to get around and reduces your mobility. Aristotle taught us that nature abhors a vacuum. Clutter expands to fill available space, and so does technology. The larger the briefcase you start with, the more crap you will likely pack. Start with a smaller case and try to not fill it up, while still packing sufficient equipment to meet your needs on the road.

Blogging Is Good ...

Blogging can be a great tool for promoting your law practice. With a well-thought-out blog, you maintain a strong online presence and can leave potential clients with a positive impression of your competency. Many lawyers who publish blogs are becoming known as experts in the area they market themselves in; it is one of the most effective ways to develop your niche. Some of the top reasons to start a blog include:

- **Exposure**. A well-maintained blog will expand your Web presence and establish you as an expert.
- **Branding**. Your professional brand highlights the unique value that sets you apart from other attorneys within your niche.
- **Attract new clients**. The days of pulling out the yellow pages and flipping to the "Lawyers" section are almost gone. Today, clients seeking legal help tend to turn to search engines like Google. A blog is a great way to gain the attention of prospective clients and convince them that you are the person to hire.
- **Generate new opportunities**. The more you develop your blog, the more people will learn about you and your organization. A thoughtful blog can open doors to new opportunities such as speaking engagements, job leads, invitations to conferences, writing opportunities with other publications, guest-blogging gigs, book deals, and a host of other opportunities that might not have found you if you did not blog.

Starting a blog takes time and thoughtful planning. Some points to consider before you get started:

- **Identify who your audience will be**. You may be targeting this marketing tool to current clients, prospective clients, lawyers in your practice area, or the general lawyer population. You may be best served by targeting all four of these potential audiences. You can aim for content that applies to all or rotate your target buy time for new developments that are relevant to each audience.

- **Start off with a private trial run to ensure you have the time to devote the attention your blog needs**.
  There are several sites where you can set up a blog quickly and start posting content before the site goes live. Try it out for a little while and see if you can afford the time commitment. If you can handle it, take the blog live.

If the time commitment is too great, or if writing is not something you particularly enjoy, then blogging may not be the best route for you. Fear not, there are still several other social media marketing tools that can be effective with less time constraints.

... Blogging with Graphics Is Better

Blog posts are good, but blog posts with graphics are better. Simply put, posts with graphics tend to be easier to read, ultimately leading to more shares, giving you more bang for your marketing buck. Graphics are useful for illustrating important points to your readers, breaking up text to make content easier to read, and can make social shares of your post stand out in a news feed.

There is no need to panic: with a few tips you can be well on your way to creating unique graphics to pair with your blog for that added oomph.

- **Find good photos**. There are tons of sources for photos out there; some are free, and some require a small fee for use. Some require that you attribute to the original author, so make sure you check the requirements before you use an image. You might want to start with:
  - www.freeimages.com
  - www.unsplash.com
  - Flickr Creative Commons
- **Use effective screenshots**. If the content you are posting includes tutorial or how-to information, you can get a lot from a screenshot. You can take screenshots from within Microsoft Word or OneNote. There are free tools like Jing that will allow you to not only capture screenshots but also easily annotate them.
- **Try Canva**. Canva is free design software. Some of the graphics or images you use can cost around $1. With Canva, you can adjust the graphics with text, backgrounds, and custom layouts to enhance your blog content. Signing up and getting started is very fast and easy. Canva begins with a 25-second tutorial that gives you all the information you need to know to be on your way. You can also upload your own photos and use its design tools. With this website and a few choice images from freeimages.com or unsplash .com, you have all the tools you need to create some great, unique graphics for your blog posts.

Embrace the Cloud

One of the easiest ways to have significant geographic redundancy in your backup plan is to store an encrypted and password-protected copy of your files in the cloud. Most commercial providers employ geographic redundancy themselves, giving you even more protection.

The cloud not only offers the opportunity for a secure and geographically redundant backup of all of your data, it provides you with opportunities for synchronization of data among multiple devices and for sharing information among a group of coworkers or others collaborating from geographically disparate locations.

We believe that every backup plan should include a copy of data that you store in the cloud. Recognize that the process of moving data in and out of the cloud works much more slowly than copying to and from a local hard disk, so you will want to have both.

Properly and safely used, the cloud can make your work and your life considerably easier and more secure.

Keep in Sync with Dropbox

Dropbox (www.dropbox.com) provides one of the many services that allow you to back up information in the cloud. By installing it on multiple computers and linking those computers to the same account, you can keep the information in the Dropbox folder synchronized to all of those computers. The process occurs automatically, as long as you leave the computers turned on and connected to the Internet. If you turn off a computer or it has no Internet connection, it can automatically start the update process as soon as you turn it back on and connectivity is restored.

You can also add Dropbox to tablets and smartphones and access the information in the Dropbox folder from those devices.

Dropbox also affords the ability to share folders inside your Dropbox folder with others who do not have general access to your Dropbox folder or to other content in that folder.

In the past, Dropbox has had some security issues. They seem to have solved those problems, but as a precaution, we recommend that you encrypt important and confidential data before storing it in Dropbox (or anywhere else in the cloud).

Dropbox offers a basic account with relatively limited storage free to everyone. Should you need more storage for your data, you can rent it for a fee.

The Pomodoro Technique

The Pomodoro Technique is a time management method developed by Francesco Cirillo. The technique involves breaking tasks into work intervals of 25 minutes each with short (five to ten minutes) breaks in between each interval. The idea behind this technique is to maximize your focus while getting a project done and reduce the mental stress of interruptions.

The method is fairly simple. You work for 25 minutes and then take a five-minute break. After four cycles of 25 minutes of work and five minutes of breaks have passed, you then take a 15- to 20-minute break. The frequent breaks will help you stay focused, and knowing you will stop in a little while and have time to check e-mail or the Internet, may make it easier to stay on task and finish a few things. Breaking tasks up in to 25-minute intervals may make billing easier too.

Benefits of this technique include that it's free and you can use any timer program on your computer or phone. If you go to the website, you can order your own pomodoro-shaped timer to use (if you find yourself in need of a kitchen timer, it can serve a dual purpose).

The technique is not flawless, and it will not stop someone from barging into your office to discuss an off-task item of business, nor will it prevent people from interrupting your brief break periods with work, but if it prompts you to finish items a little bit faster, or helps break the distracting habits getting in your way, then it is worth a try, right?

Amazon.com and Other Online Shopping Sites

The only thing better than window-shopping is anytime, anywhere, desktop window-shopping (and maybe a limitless credit card that somebody else pays off). Until the latter becomes available, anytime, anywhere, desktop window-shopping is still pretty cool. With Amazon.com, you can find competitively priced technology buys and have them shipped right to your door. Take advantage of its Amazon Prime Service and you will find a variety of options with free second-day delivery. Amazon Prime allows you to scroll through reviews and product specifications for current models, and you can often find their older iterations through third-party vendors, if that is what you want. The second-day delivery means you'll have your purchase in your hands, oftentimes faster than you would if you planned to go to the store. How often have you told yourself, "I'll go pick that up this weekend," adding the item to the growing list of weekend stops to make before you can get to the point of relaxing? Do you remember the frustration you felt when you finally reached the store only to find out the one thing you came for was out of stock?

Some of the top reasons online shoppers look to Amazon include the following:

- Price. You can usually find better bargains on the website, although as with any store, you will want to scan all the options (including third-party vendors) for the best deal. On the bright side, you can adjust your search settings to provide the lowest-cost option to appear first.
- Customer service.
- Easy returns—one of the authors uses the website regularly for buying tech accessories and has never had a problem returning the merchandise if the purchase did not work or fit as it claimed to on the website.

Afraid you might not like the product you picked out online? Amazon has a pretty consumer-friendly return policy. You can return any new, unopened items sold and fulfilled by Amazon.com within 30 days of delivery for a full refund. Amazon will even cover the cost of shipping. If you are purchasing an item from a third-party vendor through Amazon.com, you will need to read their return policy prior to ordering.

In addition to Amazon, you may want to point your browser to CDW, Newegg, and Tiger Direct for product and price comparisons. You can shop around at four different stores during a single lunch hour without ever leaving your office.

Store Data in the Cloud

Cloud computing is the process of storing and accessing your data (documents, images, spreadsheets, etc.) and sometimes your program applications over the Internet instead of on an internal drive on your computer or an external hard drive connected to your computer. The cloud is simply another way of saying "the Internet." One major benefit of storing your data (documents, images, PDFs, etc.) in the cloud is that you do not have to carry it with you, but you can get to it wherever you can access the Internet.

You should ask yourself if your data will be secure in the cloud. The answer depends on the precautions you take; properly secured data is safe. To properly secure your data, remember to

- encrypt confidential data and
- password-protect encrypted files, and
- password protect your accounts and devices.

These measures will reduce your risk of data theft.

There have been a handful of ethical opinions concerning the topic of cloud storage. As attorneys, we have ethical obligations when storing client data in the cloud. In simplified terms, you should recognize that your obligations require that you maintain a working understanding of technology and the ways that technology can help or hinder your client. You also have an obligation to take reasonable measures to safeguard your client's confidential information. Those reasonable measures will change as the technology to secure data changes. That is one of the reasons that you must maintain your knowledge of technology on a current basis.

Get a Handwriting Font

Use it to do any number of things:

- Sign e-mails.
- Sign letters.
- Sign documents.
- Send informal notes.
- Make an Acrobat signature stamp.

Fonts are Mac and Windows compatible. If you have poor handwriting and want to impress people, you might want to avoid using your own writing for the font and borrow someone else's handwriting. Alternatively, you can get a font designed by a font designer or one created from the handwriting of some fairly famous people (some of the presidential examples include Thomas Jefferson, George Washington, Abraham Lincoln, and John Adams). Write your own Declaration of Independence or just use one to make your e-mailed or printed cursive readable. The folks at vLetter made one for me several years ago, that I continue to use (www.vletter.com).

Create an Inexpensive Electronic Signature

You can pay to have someone make a signature font for you, or you can save some money and do it yourself. It does not take much effort and is relatively easy if you follow these steps:

1. Sign your name in blue ink on white paper. Make the signature larger than normal; scaling down beats scaling up in terms of image quality.
2. Scan your signature and save as .jpg to create the basic electronic file.
3. Use software (Photoshop works nicely) to make the background transparent.
4. Drop the signature into documents before printing or e-mailing.

You can also use the signature .jpg to create an Acrobat signature stamp, making it easier to add your signature to PDF documents prior to e-mailing or printing them.

Ruby Receptionists

Ruby Receptionists offers virtual phone receptionists to answer your calls and provide limited customer service when you are unavailable. Services like Ruby Receptionists can bridge the gap while you are transitioning from a one-person show to a full ensemble. If you have too much call traffic to handle solo, but not quite enough to support a full-time receptionist, this may be the solution for you. The receptionists who answer your phone are friendly and courteous, leaving your current and potential clients with the best impression, short of getting you on the first ring. Ruby's virtual receptionists answer your calls with a personalized greeting, including a friendly "Good morning/afternoon" or "Thank you for calling," along with your company name and an offer of assistance. Although this is standard, how they answer can be customized according to your instruction. You can create scenario-specific instructions; for example, you can have messages from new clients forwarded to a specific line or e-mail. Going on vacation? You can instruct Ruby Receptionists to take messages from most clients and forward any calls from deadline-constrained clients to you directly.

If you are just starting your law practice and have not set up a phone number yet, Ruby Receptionists can provide you with a toll-free number that you can publish on your website and marketing materials. If you cease to use Ruby Receptionists' service, you can take the toll-free number with you, so you do not lose the advantage of client familiarity with it.

Receptionists are available for live phone answering from 7:00 a.m. to 8:00 p.m. Monday–Friday, which centers around the typical business hours that your callers would expect a live person to answer your phone. Outside of those times, Ruby can set up a variety of automated options, which they provide at no charge.

Ruby Receptionists may come off as pricey for a seemingly intangible service. Some folks may find it difficult to swallow paying for a receptionist that they do not actually see. Their smallest package contains 100 minutes of receptionist time for $249 per month, 200 minutes for $409 per month, and 500 minutes for $819 per month. Ruby offers a free two-week trial for you to gauge approximately how many minutes you will use.

If you decide to give Ruby Receptionists a try, you might want to combine this service with a Google Voice, RingCentral, or similar service that enables you to route calls before they go through to the virtual receptionists. That way, clients who are frequent callers will not eat up your minutes.

Use Electronic Business Cards

If you are a Microsoft Outlook user, adding an electronic business card is fairly simple. With an electronic business card attached, your e-mail recipients can right-click the card in the signature block of your e-mail (or right-click the .vcf file attachment) to save it directly to their contacts list. To start, open your Outlook and a blank e-mail. Then you can choose to create a signature or choose an existing signature to modify. From here, you can include a business card in the signature.

If you would like some help creating your electronic business card, you can download templates through Microsoft at http://office .microsoft.com/en-us/templates/results.aspx?ctags = CT010253053 &CTT = 5&origin = HA010065086.

You can add backgrounds and images to your electronic business card. In order to avoid distortion, you will want the image you select for the background to be around the same size as the electronic business card itself (around 248 pixels x 148 pixels). Once you have the image sized appropriately, use the following steps to complete your task:

1. In an open contact, double-click Electronic Business Card.
2. In the Edit Business Card dialog box, in the Card Design section, click Change.
3. Locate the picture that you want to use for the background and then double-click it.
4. Next to Layout, select Background Image.
5. Click OK.
6. Click Save and Close.

URL Shorteners

Uniform resource locators (URLs) are specific character strings that serve as a sort of website mailing address, directing you to the specific location or Web resource that you seek. As you can imagine with the number of Web addresses and resources available today, the string can get rather long. Long URLs are more likely to get broken or copied wrong, so now there are a variety of URL-shortening services out there that will allow you to paste the full address into their system, and they will create a substantially shorter URL for you to copy into e-mails or presentations.

A good URL-shortening service will also provide click-through information, valuable data to have when measuring the return on investment of your time spent posting or creating the presentations.

URL shorteners are particularly useful for social media marketing. Popular URL shorteners include the following:

- Tiny URL, www.tinyurl.com
- Bitly, www.bitly.com
- Google URL Shortener available at the Chrome Web Store (chrome.google.com).

Keep in mind, the system is not perfect. There are trade-offs to be made. Accessing a link through a URL shortener will take a little longer than if you clicked on the link directly. This is due to the extra layer the link navigates to get you to your destination.

Develop Timelines for Trial Use

Timelines offer a good way to organize factual information with a chronological baseline. In many cases, knowing how the pieces fit together in time will help you better understand your case and make it easier to present to the trier of fact. A timeline can also make it easier for the trier of fact to understand the interrelationship of the significant events in your case.

You can make timelines graphically simple or more visually complex. Each has its merits. Timelines can be easily developed with software on Mac and Windows platforms. Examples of software to develop timelines include the following:

- Windows: TimeMap
- Mac: BeeDocs Timeline or Timeline 3D
- Clarity Legal Timeline

Use Flowcharts

You have heard that a picture has the value of a thousand words. A diagram can make a big difference if you are trying to explain a procedure with multiple outcomes. A demonstrative visual aid, such as a flowchart, can bolster your trial presentation. Flowcharts are also a handy tool for explaining to clients what to expect. A flowchart is a pictorial or graphical representation of a process. The purpose is to communicate how a process works or should work without the clutter of technical jargon. It generally encompasses a start point, end point, inputs, outputs, possible paths, and the decisions that lead to these possible paths.

There are several flowchart tools out there. You can create charts using the following:

- Microsoft Word
- Microsoft PowerPoint
- LucidChart
- Microsoft Visio
- SmartDraw

Flowcharts can assist you in moving a jury through a process. You can describe the process and hope your panel is taking notes, but providing a visual is more engaging. Take a simple asset transaction. It involves flows of money and assets moving in a variety of directions among many parties. A lawyer could describe all of this in sentences, but the complicated integrated nature of the transaction becomes readily apparent when displayed as a flowchart.

Following are some tips to keep in mind when creating flowcharts:

- **Keep it simple and easy to understand**. You should focus on the most important elements of the process that you want to direct your audience's attention toward.
- **Evaluate your flowchart objectively before you present it**. Make sure it conveys the points you are intending to make. Have several nonlawyers review the chart and confirm its usefulness before you use it in trial.
- Know your court's guidelines regarding visual aids before you spend the time and money creating them.

Flowcharts are a handy business tool as well. Once your practice gets under way, it is a good idea to flowchart how client information gets into your practice and flows through it. Once you have the flowchart in place, you can identify any holes in your process or any areas where you duplicate work.

Write Better E-mails

Write your e-mail with a clear chronology of events to keep it short and readable. Organize your thoughts into a coherent narrative the same way you ask clients to tell you their story.

Avoid humor and sarcasm. People often misconstrue the tone of an e-mail, and you do not want to take the chance of being misunderstood.

Remember, e-mails may survive in ways and for times that paper mail could not and would not. Do not take unnecessary chances. Never put in an e-mail what you would not put in a letter.

Avoid hitting send too soon by waiting to add the recipients after the e-mail is finalized.

Save Yourself from That "Oh No" Moment with E-mail

Have you ever hit the send button before you meant to? Or realized an error or misunderstanding seconds after sending the e-mail out? You can save yourself the embarrassment by creating a rule in Microsoft Outlook that will hold your outgoing messages for a set amount of time (say two minutes) to hopefully give you just enough time to catch your oversight.

1. In Outlook, select File, then Info.
2. On the Account Information screen, select Manage Rules and Alerts.
3. On the Rules Wizard screen, go to the "Start from blank rule" section and select "Apply rule on messages I send."
4. On the Rules and Alerts screen, select New Rule.
5. On the next Rules Wizard screen, go to "Step 1: Select condition(s)" and check "on this computer only."
6. On the next Rules Wizard screen, go to the "Step 1: Select action(s)" section and
   a. check "defer delivery by a number of minutes";
   b. select "a number of" minutes hyperlink under Step 2 on the screen;
   c. enter the number of minutes to delay sending in the popup menu (here is where you would enter 2, or 4, however long you need that will not disrupt your workflow).
7. On the next Rules Wizard screen, go to the "Step 1: Select exception(s)" section and
   a. check "except if the subject contains specific words";
   b. select the "specific words" hyperlink in Step 2;
   c. enter the specific word(s) string in the Search Text menu (you may want a few key words you can add to the subject line that will bypass the rule).
8. Enter the specific word or phrases string in the Search Text menu on which to apply the delay exception.
9. This step is a recap of the last wizard screen, confirming the choices that you just made.

10. On the next Rules Wizard screen, you can name, finalize, and review the new rule in three easy steps.
11. Accept the final notification screen and you are done.

While not perfect (it may take you five minutes to realize your mistake), the system at least buys you some time and may reduce the number of "oh no" moments you have in your practice.

Update Your Wireless Accounts

Most of us have had various forms of wireless service for many years. Many of us have accounts with the same provider over long time periods. Providers regularly restructure their accounts to reflect changing economic models. Sometimes those restructurings are advantageous for customers, sometimes not. Remember, however, that available plans and services change over time.

It makes good sense to regularly review your service plans with your wireless provider's customer care personnel. You may find that a newer plan offers the same or more service than you currently have for less money (yes, it really happens).

For example, not that long ago, you needed a separate account for each device. Then most carriers let you buy a bucket of data and add devices to the account for nominal charges and share the data. Many carriers, for example, let you add a tablet for $10 to an existing account and share the data among several devices. Now they let you bring your whole family (sometimes, and with some carriers, friends *and* family) so that a number of people can share the same allocation of data access on a monthly basis at a reduced rate.

Review your needs and your plan at least once a year. Make sure you are getting use for your data dollars. Don't overbuy. Drop unused features.

Hire an Inexpensive Editor: WordRake

WordRake seeks to improve your writing by eliminating unnecessary words. Get a "staff editor" for $129/year (or less).

WordRake works with Microsoft Word and with Outlook. It requires an Internet connection to review your work and operates on a subscription basis. Unfortunately, WordRake only works with Windows versions of Word and Outlook at the present time (www.wordrake.com).

According to the Honorable Clarence Thomas, "I think lawyers have a professional obligation to get better at our craft, and writing better is a part of that."

Beware of LinkedIn Endorsements and Recommendations

If you actively use LinkedIn, you may have seen an e-mail at some point informing you that a contact has endorsed you for a certain skill. It seems innocent enough, but attorneys should be mindful of how their state views LinkedIn endorsements in order to avoid a potential ethical rules violation. For instance, under ABA Model Rule 7.1, a lawyer is not to make any false or misleading claims about his or her services. It appears that if a lawyer permitted a misleading endorsement to remain on his or her LinkedIn profile, even if it was someone else who posted the endorsement, it could pose a problem under Rule 7.1.

Also consider: if you, the lawyer, respond to receiving this endorsement by giving your contact a similar endorsement for his or her service, you may be coming up on a violation of Model Rule 7.2(b), which limits the lawyer's ability to give anything of value to a person for recommending the lawyer's services, except under the outlined exceptions.

It is a gray area, but worth treading over carefully.

Outsource Typing

You can find a number of good transcription services to facilitate your work. As your practice grows, this may be less costly than employing a secretary, at least until your workload hits a certain level. Rather than jump into the hiring process, you can use any dictation equipment you are comfortable with and send your files in for transcription. Most of these services provide high-quality work with a fast turnaround time. When shopping for a service, look for a service that will give you 24-hour or better turnaround time. You should also look for a service that will take your forms and use them as models for your work. For most services, the files are easily transportable by e-mail or upload.

You have many choices when it comes to such services. Things that you can consider as bases for differentiation include:

- Who owns the company?
- Where does the labor come from?
- Can you get the same people working on your files on a continuing basis?
- Can you upload formats and letterhead for them to use, or do you have to reformat and print on letterhead in your own office?
- What is the normal turnaround time?
- Does the company have support staff available 24/7/365?
- What arrangements can be made to expedite turnaround time in an urgent situation?
- What are the costs for normal and expedited turnaround?
- Work quality (you can get this from references or by setting up a trial for yourself).

One of the authors has used the services of LawDocsXpress in the past and been very satisfied with it (www.lawdocsxpress.com/).

Use Outlook's follow-Up Reminder

When you are creating an e-mail in Outlook that requires a time-sensitive response, you can add a reminder to appear on your calendar, your recipient's calendar, or both.

To set up an automatic reminder, first open up a new e-mail message and create the e-mail as you normally would. Then, locate the Follow Up menu under the Message tab.

From the drop-down Follow Up menu, choose Custom; this will allow you to create a custom reminder for yourself and/or your recipients.

You can use this feature to create a monthly reminder to e-mail your clients with an update on their matter.

Organize Your Digital Files

One great feature of digital files is the ability to search your data if you don't immediately know where to find it on your hard drive. Depending on the amount of data you have stored, though, this process can get cumbersome and time consuming rather quickly. One way around this is to organize your digital files in a consistent, logical fashion. If you have a system in place and it works for you, read no further (from this page, you should still check out the rest). If you are looking for ideas on how to organize your digital files, consider structuring it as follows:

Once you have a folder structure in place, consider naming your files with the date first. This will help with sorting and finding documents down the road. If you work on a document for multiple days, you can keep a backup of your changes this way. Your files will fall in the order they were created, or last worked on, by you. Alternatively, try labeling the file with Short Common Name—YYYY-MM-DD so all of your drafts or versions of the same document will fall together. For example, your Original Petition might be labeled OPET-2014-01-04. You could also add your client's last name or a company name if you wanted to distinguish it further—for example, Smith-OPET-2014-01-04. If you put the date first, your computer will store the documents in a chronological rather than an alphabetical order.

Make Your Website "Mobile Friendly"

Websites designed for viewing on large computer screens often do not translate well to mobile displays. Smaller screens require a different layout and setup of the content to make them look good on a mobile device. Since your website may constitute the first impression you make on a prospective client, go to the effort of making a good first impression; retool your website so that clients can view it easily on mobile devices. Remember, more and more people use mobile devices for Internet searches, and you only get one chance to make a first impression.

Move Your iTunes Library to an External Drive

Many of us have developed very large collections of digital media. While individual audio files generally do not take up a great deal of space, some formats take up considerably more than others. A single high-definition movie can take several gigabytes of space and some of us have built up a significant quantity of digital audio files in our iTunes libraries. The media library for iTunes will include movies, videos, television shows, music, audiobooks (regular books too if you use iBooks), as well as podcasts and iPad and iPhone Apps (if you have one or the other or both of those devices) and more. As a result, the size of your iTunes library can easily grow very large. It is not unusual for an iTunes library to occupy several hundred thousand gigabytes of space.

We went through a period when each generation of computers offered larger hard disks for less money, but that has changed with the recent shift to flash memory. Flash memory costs more than traditional hard disks. As a result, the size of storage drives in laptops dropped considerably (from about a terabyte to 256 GB on average) and then started rising again as flash memory grew more affordable. Still, most of us do not have several hundred gigabytes on a laptop to devote to our media library. The answer: take the media library "off campus." Move it to an external hard drive. By doing that, you keep your laptop's memory free for other things, without losing the media library's functionality. Since you can get highly portable drives with large capacity, you can easily use the same drive for backup of your computer and storage of the media library.

Moving your iTunes media file to an external drive is not difficult.

1. Copy the library to the external drive.
2. Open iTunes and go to Preferences.
3. Open the Advanced options in Preferences.
4. Go to "iTunes Media folder location" and select Change.
5. Locate the copy of the library on the external drive and select it.
6. Before you close out of Advanced Preferences, you should make sure that you checked the boxes to "Keep the iTunes Media folder organized" and "Copy files to iTunes Media folder when adding to library."
7. Close out of Preferences.

Google Search Tips

The Google search engine is a powerful tool for a variety of tasks and problems. It is widely used today for almost any searching needs. How many times have you heard someone say "just Google it"?

1. **Use the tabs.** On the top of every Google search page you see tabs with options that read: Web, Image, News, and More. Choosing one of these tabs can hone your search results to what you are looking for. If you are looking for a news article, select News; you can then further limit the range of search to a specific date range.

2. **Use quotation marks (") to find an exact phrase (e.g., "ab initio").** Using quotation marks allows you to specify the sequence that words appear in, and prevents you from getting results that focus on "ab" or "initio" alone. Unless you are in the market for an ab machine, then feel free to leave the quotes off so you can multi-task while you search.

3. **Search by file type.** Search for specific types of files, such as PDFs, PPTs, or XLS, by adding the file type: and the 3-letter file abbreviation.

4. **Quickly find the time.** In the search bar, you can type "Time Houston" or anywhere in the world you would like to know the time for and it will instantly pull it up, along with what time zone the location is in.

5. **Track your packages by typing the tracking number directly into the search box.** Track your UPS, FedEx, or USPS packages by typing the tracking number directly into the search box. The results will show you the status of your shipment.

Atwitter about Twitter?

In its study entitled *The Social Habit 2014*, Edison Research surveyed 2,023 people to explore Americans' use of digital platforms and the newest media. The survey, conducted via telephone, included those age 12 and older. Of those surveyed, 92 percent knew of Twitter. The largest demographic of Twitter users were ages 12–17 (37 percent), but that was followed closely by ages 18–24 (36 percent) and 25–34 (21 percent). The remaining 32 percent were 35 and over, with ages 65 and up representing only 3 percent of Twitter users. The survey indicates that those with years of experience to offer are not using this platform to reach out to potential clients. This is a great opportunity to showcase your knowledge.

When using Twitter or any social media to market yourself, you should focus on a select few areas to become an authority, ideally areas you are already practicing in. You can also get more mileage from your tweets by linking your Twitter and LinkedIn accounts.

Fitbit

Fitbit makes a variety of wearable body metrics trackers. Both of the authors use the Fitbit devices. One of the authors favors the Fitbit Flex ($99.95, www.fitbit.com). You can buy multiple colors of bands for the device and color-coordinate with your outfits. It will sync wirelessly with computers (you connect the wireless receiver via a USB dongle) and with many smartphones (provided you have installed the required App and turned on Bluetooth). The band measures calorie burn and activity, but you have to set it manually to record sleep. It holds a charge for about five days.

Fitbit has taken the concept of wearable tech a step further by partnering with Tory Burch to create jewelry to hold the Fitbit device instead of the wristband. You can buy the Tory Burch holders separately from the Flex on the Fitbit website or from Tory Burch's website (www.toryburch.com). The Tory Burch accessories will add $38 to $195 to the price of the Fitbit, but in the words of one female attorney we know who eschewed the simple functionality of the Fitbit Flex bracelet, "Now, that's more like it!" What could be better than wearable technology? Fashionable and wearable technology!

Fitbit also coordinates with other health-oriented programs to exchange information in order to provide you with a more comprehensive picture of your health.

Fitbit has several models of tracker available now with varying sets of features. Check out the new Fitbit Charge or the newer Fitbit Surge. These devices cost more, but offer additional features, including the ability to track sleep automatically. For those of you interested in participating in the medical research projects now being organized around the newest iteration of the iOS and the iPhone, the Fitbit devices can interact with the software that they want you to use in some of those projects.

Any.do

A user-friendly to-do list App for people on the go, Any.do may prove useful for keeping track of your to-do lists, whether it requires action today, tomorrow, or some time in the future. Training yourself to use the App regularly allows you to clear your mind of all those little things you don't necessarily need to remember right away. With the App, you can create tasks, reminders, and to-dos all in one location.

You can also use Any.do as a handy list maker. Any.do has a unique feature called the Any.do moment that encourages making a habit of reviewing your daily tasks. You can manage your family and household to-dos along with your work and team projects.

For $3/month (or $27/year), you can subscribe to the premium version. The premium version allows you to create recurring tasks and have an unlimited number of people collaborate on tasks. The free version allows collaboration but restricts you to two users per task.

There is a Web-based App for Any.do as well, allowing people to use the service anywhere they have Internet access and use a Web browser.

Trello

A free collaborative task manager App, Trello can come in very handy in helping you manage tasks or matters with a partner or staff member. The App allows you to drag and drop task cards and lists, personalize cover images, add checklists, and create new boards. To collaborate with others, just have them install Trello on their devices and set up an account, you can add users by name, and any changes you make will be synced in real time. Once all your users are added to the project, you will have a visual overview of what is being worked on and who is working on it. Oh, and did we mention that it does not cost you anything? Go to the website, set up your account and start organizing! (www.trello.com)

Trello is a project management system made up of boards, lists, and cards. This system allows teams to track a project and collaborate and readily identify where they can contribute or be most useful or where it is most needed. Project (or matter) managers can create a board for each matter that a team is handling, add your assistant(s), paralegal(s), or co-counsel to the board and create lists noting what you have "To-Do," what is "In Progress," and what is "Done." You may want a list for tasks with questions or items needing clarification so your team members can move cards there for your review when you are not at the office. You can add cards under each list for the tasks or action items and assign a team member to each card. Each team member can make notes on the progress, or add questions, or mark it as finished when complete. At the start of filing, you can create a "Deadlines" board and list out the upcoming deadlines for everyone to be aware. Trello basically acts as a whiteboard that lets you organize and create lists that work with how you think.

Get Our Books

We think we may have saved the best for last (no cliché intended). We have written and continue to write books for lawyers to help them better understand, cope with, and benefit from technology. As we consider ourselves among our favorite authors on technology and believe that you will find our books useful, we do not hesitate to recommend them to you.

Besides this book, we have two others already out: *Technology Solutions for Today's Lawyer* (American Bar Association GP Solo Division 2014) and *The iPad for Lawyers* (West 2014).

In addition to this book, we have two more in progress. They do not yet have official titles, but our working titles are *Technology and Practice Tips for Seniors* (American Bar Association Senior Lawyers Division and GP Solo Division), which will be out later this year, and *Technology for Litigators* (American Bar Association GP Solo Division).

Jeffrey Allen
jallenlawtek@aol.com
Ashley Hallene
ahallene@gmail.com